# HIKING TRAILS I

## Victoria and Vicinity

Covering the Capital Regional District
including
Portland and Sidney Islands

Published by

Vancouver Island Trails Information Society

**THIRTEENTH Edition, 2007**

Revised and edited by Richard K. Blier

**Library and Archives Canada Cataloguing in Publication**
Blier, Richard K., 1952-
Hiking trails I : Victoria and vicinity / compiled and edited
by Richard K. Blier. — 13th ed.
Includes index.
ISBN10  0-9697667-5-0
ISBN13  978 0-9697667-5-9
1. Hiking—British Columbia—Victoria Region—Guidebooks.
2. Trails—British Columbia—Victoria Region—Guidebooks.
3. Victoria Region (B.C.)—Guidebooks. I. Vancouver Island Trails Information
Society II. Title.
FC3844.2.H54 2006 917.11'28045 C2006-903544-X

Cover photograph:  East Sooke Park, Permission of Maggie Birchmore

This edition is dedicated to Ronald J. Weir,
whose knowledge and counsel
guided our committee for many years.

Ron gave freely of his time and energy to preserve
and protect land, trails and heritage in the Metchosin
and Sooke Area. He was a gentleman whose advice
was valued by so many.

# Preface

This southern Vancouver Island area is blessed with a mild climate that invites year round hiking. It is also endowed with a multitude of parks and open spaces (a conservative estimate is 500) and is the home of a populace who places these attributes and outdoor recreation at the top of its priorities.

*Hiking Trails I* features a variety of over 100 walks and hikes. Most are within a short drive of downtown or home. Pick a hike that suits the ability and timetable of you and your family. You will find short walks in small, nearby parks and longer hikes in larger more distant parks. Walks around our lakes and nature sanctuaries are generally quite level and easy.

There is no shortage of local hills to give you a good workout and to reward you with views of the Saanich Peninsula, downtown Victoria, the Canadian Gulf Islands and the American San Juan Islands. All this is enclosed in a necklace of magnificent distant mountain ranges. To the northeast, rises British Columbia's Coast Mountain range, revealing areas beyond Vancouver and the Fraser Valley. Directly east, is the Cascade Range in Washington State with the craggy peaks of the Skagit Valley and Mount Baker; and in the southeast you may find Mount Rainier on a really clear day, if you look to where the Olympic Mountains dip into Puget Sound. South, across Juan de Fuca Strait, is the Olympic Mountain Range, full of snowcapped peaks and backcountry, with alpine hiking opportunities. Far to the west is Neah Bay, Cape Flattery and the open Pacific Ocean.

This **Thirteenth Edition** of *Hiking Trails I* aims to preserve the achievements of the previous editions in making hiking trail information easy to find and use. It retains popular features such as Arnold Fraser's beautifully drawn maps, original sketches used in all three books and some new maps used with the permission of the Capital Regional District and Saanich Parks.

Each hiking trail is now described using a uniform presentation. This format begins with the highlights of the main hiking trail, rates its degree of difficulty, gives directions on how to find the trailhead, follows with a generalized description and concludes with comments about noteworthy aspects of the trail/park. At the end of each hike description, there is a short section about nearby nature parks or walks with points of interest that are worth visiting, time and energy permitting.

Park agencies and municipalities provide nature programs and guided walks for families and children as well as publishing a myriad of brochures.

Some of their website pages are listed in Information Sources, (page 167) and on our website: hikingtrailsbooks.com.

The selection of hikes you will find in this volume will introduce you to southern Vancouver Island's best nature parks, with areas of significant natural beauty, fauna and flora. These are the hikes, parks and open spaces that the efforts of dedicated people such as Ron Weir, to whom this edition is dedicated, have preserved from development forever. Go and enjoy them.

**George Broome**
**Vancouver Island Trails Information Society**

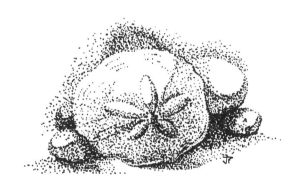

# CONTENTS

Preface . . . . . . . . . . . . . . . . . . . . . . . . . . . . . 4

Map and Key to Hiking Areas . . . . . . . . . . . . . . . . . 9

Legend . . . . . . . . . . . . . . . . . . . . . . . . . . . . . . 10

How to Use This Book . . . . . . . . . . . . . . . . . . . . 11

Hints and Cautions . . . . . . . . . . . . . . . . . . . . . . . 13

Vancouver Island Trails Information Society . . . . . . . . . 19

1.  Portland Island . . . . . . . . . . . . . . . . . . . . . . . 20

2.  Sidney Island . . . . . . . . . . . . . . . . . . . . . . . . 24
    D'Arcy Island

3.  Horth Hill . . . . . . . . . . . . . . . . . . . . . . . . . 28
    Green Park

4.  John Dean . . . . . . . . . . . . . . . . . . . . . . . . . 32
    Dominion Brook, Coles Bay

5.  Gowlland Tod . . . . . . . . . . . . . . . . . . . . . . . 36
    Tod Inlet, Oak Haven, Gore Park

6.  Mount Work . . . . . . . . . . . . . . . . . . . . . . . . 42
    McKenzie Bight

7.  Lone Tree Hill . . . . . . . . . . . . . . . . . . . . . . . 46

8.  Goldstream/Mount Finlayson . . . . . . . . . . . . . . . 48

9.  Francis/King . . . . . . . . . . . . . . . . . . . . . . . . 52

10. Elk/Beaver Lake . . . . . . . . . . . . . . . . . . . . . . 56
    Bear Hill

11. Rithet's Bog . . . . . . . . . . . . . . . . . . . . . . . . 60
    Rolston Trail

12  Mount Douglas . . . . . . . . . . . . . . . . . . . . . . 62
    Glencoe Cove-Kwatsech, Arbutus Cove

13. University of Victoria . . . . . . . . . . . . . . . . . . . 68
    Mount Tolmie, Mystic Vale

14  Cedar Hill Golf Course . . . . . . . . . . . . . . . . . . 72

15. Victoria Waterfront . . . . . . . . . . . . . . . . . . . . 74
    Ogden Point to Oak Bay, Ogden Point to West Bay

16  Swan Lake and Christmas Hill . . . . . . . . . . . . . . 78
    Playfair, Beckwith Park

Contents

17  Colquitz River . . . . . . . . . . . . . . . . . . . . . . . . . 82
    Cuthbert Holmes, Swan Creek, Knockan Hill,
    Layritz, Quick's Bottom

18  Thetis Lake . . . . . . . . . . . . . . . . . . . . . . . . . . 86

19  Mill Hill . . . . . . . . . . . . . . . . . . . . . . . . . . . . 90

20  Mount Wells. . . . . . . . . . . . . . . . . . . . . . . . . . 94
    Sooke Hills Wilderness Reserve

21. Metchosin Shoreline. . . . . . . . . . . . . . . . . . . . . 98
    Albert Head Lagoon, Witty's Lagoon
    Sea Bluff Trail, Devonian

22  Western Metchosin  . . . . . . . . . . . . . . . . . . . . . 104
    Matheson Lake, Roche Cove, Blinkhorn Lake,
    Metchosin Wilderness, Elizabeth Mann,
    Buckbrush Swamp, Bob Mountain, Wayne's Rock

23  East Sooke . . . . . . . . . . . . . . . . . . . . . . . . . . 112

24. Whiffin Spit . . . . . . . . . . . . . . . . . . . . . . . . . 120

25  Sooke Potholes. . . . . . . . . . . . . . . . . . . . . . . . 124
    Sooke Mountain

26  West Coast Road: Sooke to Port Renfrew . . . . . . . . . . 130

R27 Juan de Fuca Trail . . . . . . . . . . . . . . . . . . . . . 140

R28 Galloping Goose Trail . . . . . . . . . . . . . . . . . . . 146

R29 Lochside Trail . . . . . . . . . . . . . . . . . . . . . . . 152

Campgrounds . . . . . . . . . . . . . . . . . . . . . . . . . . 157

Accessible Areas. . . . . . . . . . . . . . . . . . . . . . . . . 158

Nature Walks . . . . . . . . . . . . . . . . . . . . . . . . . . 160

Birdwatching . . . . . . . . . . . . . . . . . . . . . . . . . . 162

Suggested Reading . . . . . . . . . . . . . . . . . . . . . . . 165

Information Sources . . . . . . . . . . . . . . . . . . . . . . . 167

List of Maps . . . . . . . . . . . . . . . . . . . . . . . . . . 168

Acknowledgements . . . . . . . . . . . . . . . . . . . . . . . 169

Postscript . . . . . . . . . . . . . . . . . . . . . . . . . . . . 170

About the Editor. . . . . . . . . . . . . . . . . . . . . . . . . 171

Index . . . . . . . . . . . . . . . . . . . . . . . . . . . . . . 172

## Map and Key to Hiking Areas

| | |
|---|---|
| 1. Portland Island . . . . . . . 20 | 16. Swan Lake & Christmas Hill . . 78 |
| 2. Sidney Spit . . . . . . . . . 24 | 17. Colquitz River . . . . . . . . 82 |
| 3. Horth Hill . . . . . . . . . . 28 | 18. Thetis Lake . . . . . . . . . . 86 |
| 4. John Dean . . . . . . . . . . 32 | 19. Mill Hill . . . . . . . . . . 90 |
| 5. Gowlland Tod . . . . . . . 36 | 20. Mount Wells . . . . . . . . 94 |
| 6. Mount Work . . . . . . . . . 42 | 21. Metchosin Shoreline . . . . . 98 |
| 7. Lone Tree Hill . . . . . . . . 46 | 22. Western Metchosin . . . . . 104 |
| 8. Goldstream/Mount Finlayson . 48 | 23. East Sooke . . . . . . . . . 112 |
| 9. Francis/King . . . . . . . . . 52 | 24. Whiffin Spit . . . . . . . . . 120 |
| 10. Elk/Beaver Lake . . . . . . 56 | 25. Sooke Potholes . . . . . . . 124 |
| 11. Rithet's Bog . . . . . . . . 60 | 26. West Coast Road: Sooke to |
| 12. Mount Douglas . . . . . . . 62 | Port Renfrew . . . . . . . 130 |
| 13. University of Victoria . . . . 68 | R27. Juan de Fuca Trail . . . . . 140 |
| 14. Cedar Hill Golf Course . . . . 72 | R28 Galloping Goose Trail . . . 146 |
| 15. Victoria Waterfront . . . . . 74 | R29. Lochside Trail . . . . . . . 152 |

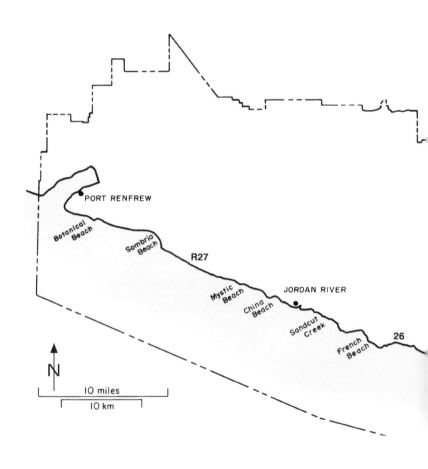

# Map and Key to Hiking Areas

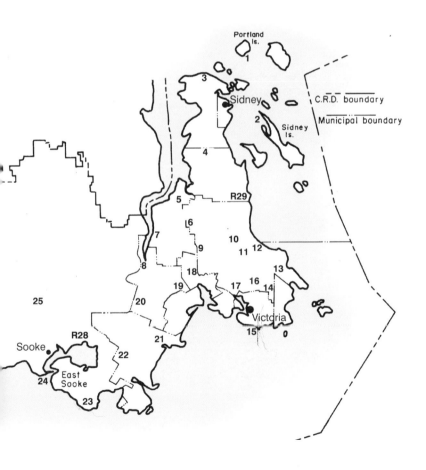

# Map Legend

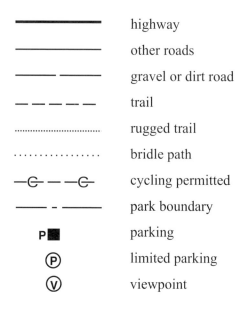

| | |
|---|---|
| ———————— | highway |
| ———————— | other roads |
| ——— ——— | gravel or dirt road |
| — — — — — | trail |
| ································· | rugged trail |
| · · · · · · · · · · · · · · · · | bridle path |
| —C— — —C— | cycling permitted |
| ——— · ——— | park boundary |
| P▓ | parking |
| Ⓟ | limited parking |
| Ⓥ | viewpoint |

Trails highlighted on the map are mentioned in the text.

Note that maps are not all at the same scale.

Toilet facilities and picnic tables are not shown on the maps. These are termed "park facilities" and will usually be found near the main parking area.

# How To Use This Book

*Hiking Trails I* is divided into 29 hiking areas. In most cases you will find more than one choice of trails. Note: An "R" preceding a number/section/listing denotes "Regional Trail".

**Maps:** Hiking areas are accompanied by their own maps. In a few cases, maps are not required. A list of maps is found on page 168.

**Highlights:** A brief summary of what the hike offers, what you will discover in the area and scenic highlights.

**Difficulty – Easy:** The trail is generally level with little or no elevation gain or hills. The trail's surface may be paved, boardwalk, gravel, chip or dirt.

**Difficulty – Moderate:** These trails may be muddy and uneven, with roots and branches, elevation changes, creek crossings and some steep hills.

**Difficulty – Strenuous:** On these trails expect frequent elevation changes and long, steep hills. You may encounter slick logs, blowdowns and tricky creek crossings. Trails may be narrow, rough and uneven. These routes are prone to slippery, muddy conditions and are often less maintained and sometimes overgrown. These trails traverse difficult, more remote terrain and may not be suitable for children or inexperienced hikers.

**Distances:** Wherever possible one-way (or loop) hiking distances are noted. Occasionally average hiking times are listed. These are subjective ratings and hiking times will depend on an individual's pace, one's degree of fitness, the trail's condition, the weather and the time of year. Use these as general guides only.

**Legend:** For map symbols see page 10.

**Cautions:** Here you may find information on trail hazards, potential problem spots, localized conditions and other things to watch out for and know prior to your hike.

**Access:** Concise directions to area trailheads is found under this heading.

**Hike Descriptions:**

The start of the hike descriptions are identified by the hiker in the margin and the featured hikes are described in detail.

**Worth Noting:** Here you may find facts on plants, animals, birds and land forms. Area background information, historical notes, local regulations and restrictions, and hints will help to ensure your hike is a safe, enjoyable one.

**Nearby:** This section briefly describes some additional parks, trails and points of interest close to the featured area.

**Additional Resources and Information:** This can be found starting on page 157 or watch for the latest relevant information on our website: hikingtrailsbooks.com.

## Warning - Disclaimer

It is necessary that all persons take responsibility for their own actions. The Vancouver Island Trails Information Society will not be liable for any mishap occurring as a consequence of any misunderstanding or misinterpretation of any content of this book or for any errors or omissions.

# Hints and Cautions

The trails in this book are either under municipal, regional, provincial or federal park administration. Where a park agency has any safety concerns there will generally be warning signs. Do not ignore them.

Each hike described in this book contains precautionary notes and reminders of some of the advice found in this section. Not all will apply to short day walks.

The following preparations and precautions are suggested:

**Trip Planning**

- Tell your family or a close friend where you are going, with whom and when you expect to return. Leave a note on your notice board, in your appointment calendar or desk diary, or even a short phone message.
- Do not hike alone. Take one or more companions.
- Start your hike early in the day, to enjoy the cool of the morning, and plan to finish early. This will give you a safe margin of time to deal with any unforeseen experiences.
- If you are new to the community, join a hiking club or group. Many community recreation centres and the YM/YWCA include hiking programs in their recreation schedules.
- Hiking with a group allows you to hike trails that require a vehicle to be parked at both ends of the trail, such as the coast trail in East Sooke Regional Park, or the hike from Goldstream Park over Mount Finlayson, and finishing in the Mount Work/Gowlland Tod parking lot on Ross-Durrance Lake Road.

**Weather**

Check the weather forecast before setting out, but remember that weather can change unexpectedly. A fine, warm sunny day can turn wild, wet and windy with little forewarning. Cold, damp fogs may be experienced even in the summer, and they can be accompanied by strong, cold westerly winds in the Juan de Fuca Strait. Hilltops are more exposed to wind, and temperatures can be several degrees cooler.

**Dress and Footwear**

- Dress in several light layers to allow you to add clothing to stay warm or to take some off to remain cool.
- Carry a good rain suit.
- Wear comfortable hiking boots or walking shoes. Break in new footwear on short walks and hikes.

- Gaiters will stop water, sticks and stones from getting into your boots when hiking in wet and muddy conditions, and prevent ticks attaching themselves to your ankles.
- Use a hiking stick on the more rugged trails. The use of two light, collapsible hiking poles is gaining popularity.
- Leave a change of dry clothing in the trunk of your car for your return.

**What to carry in your day pack:**
- Hat, gloves and extra clothing
- Rain jacket and pants (for windy as well as rainy conditions)
- Sunglasses and sunscreen
- *Hiking Trails I* or trail map
- Compass and/or GPS unit
- Pocket knife
- Flagging tape or biodegradable alternate
- Whistle and signalling mirror
- Flashlight and spare batteries
- Candle and waterproof matches or lighter
- Cell phone (which may be of limited use)
- A small plastic bag for garbage
- An emergency space blanket
- A large orange plastic bag
- Food, drink and snacks
- Identification in case of an accident

**A First Aid Kit to keep in your day pack or car should contain:**
- Moleskin (to protect against blisters)
- Needle and tweezers for splinters
- Antihistamine for reactions to bites and stings or your personal allergy prescription
- Insect repellent and after bite treatment
- Tube of antibiotic ointment
- Band-aids for scrapes and cuts
- Tensor and finger bandage for sprains
- Water purification tablets

**Bite, Sting and Tick Prevention**

- Wear white or light-coloured fabrics.
- Avoid the use of perfumes.
- Apply an insect repellent according to the directions.

**Food, Drink and Trail Snacks**
On a half-day outing carry a bottle of water and trail-mix (nuts, raisins and chocolate) or energy bars to snack on. If you are out for the day, pack a lunch (sandwiches, cheese and crackers and fresh fruit). Carry more rather than less. Do not drink untreated stream water.

**Extras**
Camera, binoculars, natural history guidebook.

**Waterproofing Tip**
Articles placed in an orange-coloured plastic garbage bag inside your pack sack will remain dry in the wettest weather and it can be used as a distress signal in an emergency.

**Avoiding getting lost**
Stay on the main trail. Housing developments now border on nearly all park boundaries, and unplanned, unwanted trails from these properties are an unfortunate consequence. If you are uncertain as to which is the proper route, take your time in deciding which one to follow.

Look around for trail flagging (usually red). Get in the habit of occasionally looking back to see how the trail will look on the return hike. Use flagging tape or a biodegradable alternative at trail intersections to indicate your return route.

**Getting 'Un-lost'**
If you feel lost, stop hiking. Stay calm. Often this is all it takes to find your bearings. Gauge the amount of daylight remaining and prepare to spend the night outdoors if necessary. Come daylight, move to open ground where air or ground searchers can spot you. Signal your position by blowing your whistle and tie your orange emergency bag in a place where it can be seen from the air. Use your cellphone if you are carrying one.

**Avoiding Falls**
Going uphill is generally easier and safer than coming down. On hikes that include hill climbs, take your time. Descend slowly and cautiously. Beware of loose stones, moss covered rocks, protruding tree roots, wet logs and especially arbutus leaves. Help each other in areas where you feel insecure.

## Hypothermia

A combination of wet and wind can lead to hypothermia, a lowering of the body's core temperature that brings on uncontrolled shivering, forgetfulness, malaise and reluctance to keep moving. Stay warm, add a layer of clothing if the temperature drops and you feel cool. Stay dry, put your rain gear on at the earliest opportunity.

## Hyperthermia (Heat exhaustion and heat stroke)

Hyperthermia is overheating of the body core brought on in warm weather by vigorous exercise and several contributory factors. On your hikes, drink plenty of water, wear a hat to shade your head, dress lightly (shed excess layers of clothing), and rest frequently in shady spots.

## Bears and Cougars

On many trails you will be hiking in bear and cougar territory. Bear sightings are rare, and cougar sightings are especially rare. Attacks are extremely rare. Bears and cougars will sense you before you sense them. They will avoid you.

## Suggestions:

- Leave your pet at home.
- Attach a bell or noisemaker to your pack, walking stick or clothing.
- Talk a lot and make noise.
- Watch for signs such as droppings and tracks.
- Be careful around berry patches and streams with spawning salmon.
- Do not let children wander, run ahead or lag behind.
- Never approach bear cubs or cougar kittens.
- Never get between them and their mother.
- Do not wear scented cosmetics, hair spray or deodorants.
- If you come upon a fresh kill, leave the area immediately.
- If you encounter a bear:
  - Stay calm.
  - Do not do anything suddenly.
  - Do not turn and run, back away slowly.
  - Do not shout, talk calmly to it.
  - Do not wave your arms about.
- If you encounter a cougar:
  - Stay calm.
  - Give the cougar an escape route.
  - Make yourself look big and aggressive.

- Do not turn and run, back away slowly.
- Shout and make noise.
- Wave your arms and hiking stick.
- Report the sighting to the park authority, conservation officer or police.

**Snakes**
There are no poisonous snakes on Vancouver Island.

**Bus services**
Buses will take you to most of these hikes. Bus schedules can be picked up on the buses or contact BC Transit.

**Driving Directions**
Driving directions all start from downtown Victoria. For detailed road information, use a Victoria area street map.

**Parking**
Park only in designated areas. If parking on the roadside, be sure to check for restrictions.

Automobile break-ins are an unfortunate possibility. Leave valuable items at home or keep them with you. If you leave anything in your car, lock it in the trunk. Leave nothing on your vehicle dashboard or on the seats where it can be seen.

**Dog Regulations**

- Dogs are welcome in most regional parks and trails.
- Nearly all parks require dogs to be leashed.
- Specific information on these requirements will be posted on the notice board at each park.
- Dogs should be on a short leash for good control.
- Unleashed dogs may chase wildlife and damage fragile ecosystems.
- Not all humans are comfortable in the presence of dogs.
- Droppings should be picked up and removed from the trail side.

**Fires**
Fires are not permitted in most parks and are generally not necessary on a day hike. Fires are usually banned in the summer because of the very dry conditions. If you see a fire, report it at once. Dial zero and ask for Zenith-5555, or dial direct to 1-800-663-5555 (*5555 for a Cell Phone).

**Smoking**

Humans cause sixty to eighty percent of forest fires. Never smoke when hiking.

**Errors, Omissions and Updates**

Conditions of the parks and trails described in this book may change. Since our books are generally only revised every three to five years, VITIS has a website where additional information can be posted. We ask that you help us to keep our information accurate and useful by contacting us at our website: hikingtrailsbooks.com or by toll free phone: 1-866-598-0003. All park agencies maintain websites with current information about parks and outdoor recreation or they can be reached by telephone, with numbers listed in the Governments section of the telephone directory. Telephone numbers are also usually listed on park information boards.

---

**Responsible Hiking**

Before starting your hike, check the park's information board to learn about any special rules and regulations and any safety issues, such as a bear or cougar sighting. Make a note of the phone number for reporting incidents.

- Plan and prepare for your hike. Research the area if necessary.

- Obey all park rules and regulations.

- Protect the environment by staying on the trails. Do not disturb plants or wildflowers, or damage trees and any of the natural surroundings.

- Pack out what you pack in. Leave nothing and take nothing.

- Respect private property. Ask for permission to enter. Close gates that were closed; leave open those that were open.

---

**George Broome**
**Vancouver Island Trails Information Society**

## Vancouver Island Trails Information Society

The Vancouver Island Trails Information Society is a non-profit society dedicated to providing accurate information to the public about parks and trails on Vancouver Island. The object of the society is to increase the interest of the general public in the outdoors and in hiking, by publishing information relating to these activities.

The first edition of *Hiking Trails I, Victoria & Vicinity*, was published in 1972, followed by *Hiking Trails II, Southeastern Vancouver Island* in 1973 and *Hiking Trails III, North Vancouver Island*, including Strathcona Park in 1975. Originally the society was formed as the Outdoor Club of Victoria Trails Information Society under the direction and leadership of Editor, Jane Waddell Renaud. In 1993, to eliminate confusion, the society changed its name to the Vancouver Island Trails Information Society. Our society has an unbroken 35-year history of producing hiking trails books covering all of Vancouver Island. We also maintain an up-to-date web site with additional support and resource information. Our volunteer members maintain the operation of the society and guide the production of the Hiking Trails books.

Information is gathered with the assistance of dedicated hikers and climbers who have contributed accurate descriptions of trail conditions, suggested corrections and pointed the way to new hiking destinations. Agencies such as BC Parks, Capitol Regional District and others have also provided helpful information.

For more information about VITIS

e-mail: **trails@hikingtrailsbooks.com**
or visit
website: **hikingtrailsbooks.com**
telephone: toll free 1-866-598-0003
fax: toll free 1-866-474-4577

# 1. Portland Island

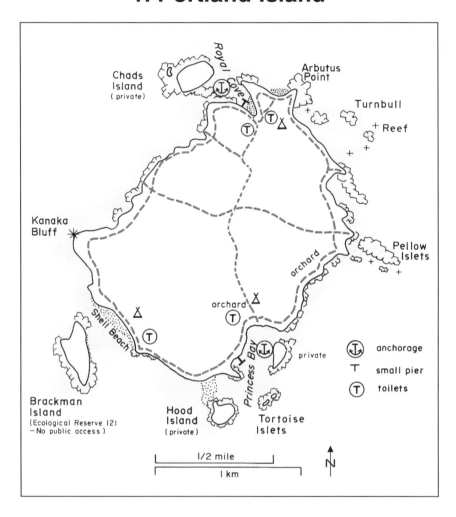

Chads Island ( private )

Arbutus Point

Turnbull

+ Reef

Kanaka Bluff

Pellow Islets

orchard

orchard

private

Brackman Island (Ecological Reserve 121 — No public access )

Hood Island ( private )

Tortoise Islets

- ⚓ anchorage
- T small pier
- Ⓣ toilets

1/2 mile

1 km

N

# 1. Portland Island

**Highlights:** Portland Island (194 ha), northeast of the town of Sidney, features a network of trails, including an up-and-down coastal route, that lead to spectacular seascapes, pocket beaches and excellent opportunities for wildlife viewing.

**Difficulty/Distance:** moderate/up to 6.5 km loop

**Access:** Portland Island is only accessible by boat or pre-booked water taxi service from Sidney, landing at Princess Bay. There is no scheduled ferry service. For more information and current park fees contact Parks Canada. (See page 167.)

**Hike Descriptions:**

**Portland Island**, part of Parks Canada's Gulf Islands National Park Reserve, is largely undeveloped. There are well-established, signposted trails that criss-cross and circle the island. The inland trails wind through forests of arbutus and Garry oak.

The most popular hike follows the rugged coast trail and snakes almost 6.5 km around the island. If your time is limited, explore only part of the shoreline. Between Princess Bay and Arbutus Point there are plenty of seascapes, tiny bays and pocket coves, shell beaches, wave-etched sandstone rocks and bluffs. The offshore Pellow Islets and the section of bluff trail near Arbutus Point are highlights.

Portland Island has an abundance of wildlife. Watch for Red-tailed Hawks, Bald Eagles and Turkey Vultures soaring overhead. Scan shoreline shallows for foraging Oystercatchers or Great Blue Herons. The waters near offshore islands are where to look for harbour seals. If you are lucky you may see these animals hauled-out on tide-exposed rocks. The island is home to black-tail deer, river otters, mink and many raccoon.

The park's shell middens (refuse piles) date back 3000 years and attest to early native use of the island. These protected archaeological sites should not be disturbed. On the island's southeast side are the remnants of two old orchards.

**Worth Noting:**
- Pack out all your garbage.
- Camping is permitted in three designated areas: Princess Bay, Shell Beach and Arbutus Point. Princess Bay and Royal Cove provide good seasonal anchorage. Best swimming is at Princess Bay's shell beach.

- The smaller islands around Portland Island (Hood Island, the Tortoise Islets and Chad Island) are privately owned. Do not trespass. There is no public access on Brackman Island, an ecological reserve.
- In 1991 the freighter MV *G.B. Church* was sunk off Portland Island's northeast shore to become BC's first artificial reef.

**Portland Island** was officially named in 1858 after the flagship HMS *Portland*. In 1875, John Palau from the Sandwich Islands (now Hawaii) pre-empted land here. Kanakas (Hawaiians) were numerous among early Hudson Bay Company workers all along our coast. This may account for the names Kanaka Bluff and Pellow Islets.

~ ~ ~

In the late 1920s, "One-armed Sutton", a colourful character who had served at Gallipoli, China, South America and Mexico, won a Derby Sweep Stake and bought the island, with ambitious plans. He built a racing horse stable, planted an orchard with apple and plum trees near Princess Bay and had pens built to house Chinese pheasants. The 1929 Wall Street crash wrecked his plans and he forfeited Portland Island. In 1944, after many changes of fortune, he died destitute in a Japanese prison camp in Hong Kong.

~ ~ ~

Portland Island was presented to Princess Margaret in 1958 and she graciously returned it in 1967 "for the benefit of the people of the province". It became Princess Margaret Provincial Marine Park. In 2003, Portland Island was incorporated into Parks Canada's Gulf Islands National Park Reserve.

**Cormorants**

On your trip over to Portland and Sidney Islands, watch for cormorants, an easily identified and common diving sea bird. They may fly low over the water and will often be seen standing tall on the rocks, a log or a navigation buoy holding their wings out to dry after a deep dive. They are dark goose-sized birds with long necks and bills and by absorbing water into their wing feathers they are able to dive to 46 or more metres. They usually fly in single file. Another unusual feature is that their webbed feet have four toes, which enables them to cling to vertical cliffs where they nest. The extra toe also allows them to feed on sand lance and shoaling Pacific herring.

# 2. Sidney Spit

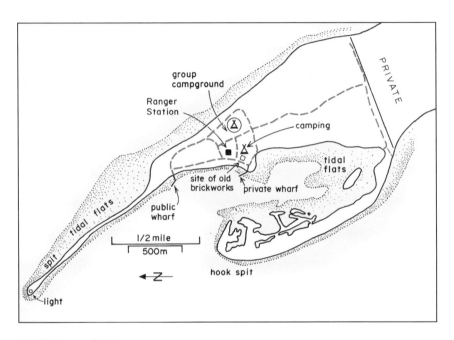

## 2. Sidney Spit

**Highlights:** Sidney Spit, situated at the northern tip of Sidney Island, lies about 5 km offshore from the town of Sidney. Formerly a provincial marine park, Sidney Spit is now part of the Gulf Islands National Park Reserve (GINPR). The 400-ha park features trails that access two long, sandy beach spits, salt marshes, a tranquil lagoon, tidal flats and scenic viewpoints. The park is renowned for its birdwatching (particularly migratory shorebirds), wildlife viewing and striking seascapes.

**Difficulty/Distance:** easy/2 km to 4.5 km, one way

**Access:** Sidney Spit, like Portland Island, is accessed by water only. A foot-passenger ferry operates from Sidney in the summer season. Check with Parks Canada for ferry schedules, current fees, accessibility and regulations. (See page 167.)

**Hike Descriptions:**

**East Beach and the Bluff** (easy/2.2 km, loop): From the public wharf the trail climbs east to the bluff. Here there are great views over Miners Channel to Mandarte and the Halibut islands. In clear weather, Mount Baker will dominate the backdrop. A set of deteriorating stairs accesses the beach. The trail parallels the bluff along Sidney Island's east side and then swings inland through uplands of arbutus and Douglas-fir, meadows and open fields. Continue past the camping areas and follow the signposts back to the public wharf, near the day-use area.

**Sidney Spit** (easy/2 km, one way): From the public wharf you can hike for 2 km, all the way to the marine navigation light at the tip of Sidney Spit. Time your hike for low tides, which expose the tidal flats and will assist your beachcombing efforts. The spectacular white sand peninsula is littered with gnarled driftwood and beach grasses and offers little protection from the sun. Gear up accordingly.

**Lagoon and Hook Spit** (easy/4.5 km, one way): From the public wharf, swing right, past West Beach and the camping area and then follow the inland trail south to the park boundary and a junction. The trail to the left goes east to the bluff that overlooks Miners Channel. Turn right and hike west. As the trail approaches tidewater, there is a short, steep hill. The head of the lagoon is a park highlight and birdwatcher's paradise. At lower tides the exposed mud flats harbour tiny Dungeness and Red Rock Crabs feeding in a dense carpet of eelgrass.

The lagoon is approximately the halfway point on the hike out to the end of the hook spit. There is another 2 km (one way) or so to go, though it looks like a shorter distance than it really is. The inner lagoon, salt marshes, tidal flats and spit are sensitive ecosystems. Parks Canada reminds visitors that access in these areas is restricted to a narrow corridor along the hook spit's outer fringe.

**Worth Noting:**

- Situated on the edge of the Pacific Flyway, Sidney Island is a superb habitat for migrating shorebirds. The lagoon is a year round birdwatching destination. Sidney Island has the southern Gulf Islands' largest Great Blue Heron colony estimated at well over 100 pairs. Brandt geese are numerous in March and April.
- On your trip over to Sidney Island watch for marine mammals, cormorants, Rhinoceros Auklets and Hermann's Gulls.
- Potable water is available but it has high sodium content. It is best to bring your own fresh water.
- The park has no garbage facilities. If you bring it in, pack it out.
- Carry a portable stove if you camp.
- Tenting is permitted in the field near the private wharf or at the inland group camping area.

**Nearby:**
**D'Arcy Island** (83 ha) is just south of Sidney Island and was once a leper colony at the turn of the 1900s. Short trails, through a forest of arbutus and Douglas-fir, lead to tiny coves and cobble beaches. D'Arcy Island is part of the GINPR.

In 1995, the Pacific Marine Heritage Legacy program began land procurement that in 2003 resulted in the creation of Canada's fifth smallest national park, the Gulf Islands National Park Reserve. Located in the southern Georgia Strait, the park reserve is made up of properties on 16 islands, over 30 reefs and islets, their adjoining waters and intertidal zones.

~ ~ ~

The bricks for Victoria's Empress Hotel were produced at the site of the old brick works, where the Sidney Island Brick and Tile Company operated from 1906 to 1915. Brick remnants are still visible along the shoreline and in the forest. Fallow deer are a common sight in the island's meadows and open grassy fields. Originally imported to nearby James Island from England at the turn of the 1900s, the deer swam to Sidney Island in the 1960s.

**Great Blue Heron**
The Great Blue Heron is another common resident of our coast. It is Canada's largest bird, standing over one metre high with a wingspan of just under two metres, but their weight rarely exceeds 2.5 kg. Herons are a gregarious species nesting in colonies, normally high in the treetops, often a long way from the water. They eat a wide variety of prey and forage day or night. They can usually be seen standing perfectly still on rocks or docks, in shallow or deep water (often up to their 'tummies') waiting for their prey to come within striking distance of their long bills. This ungainly-looking bird takes its prey with great speed. Their flexible diet makes them just as at home feeding in farm fields and meadows.

Photo: Di Chawner

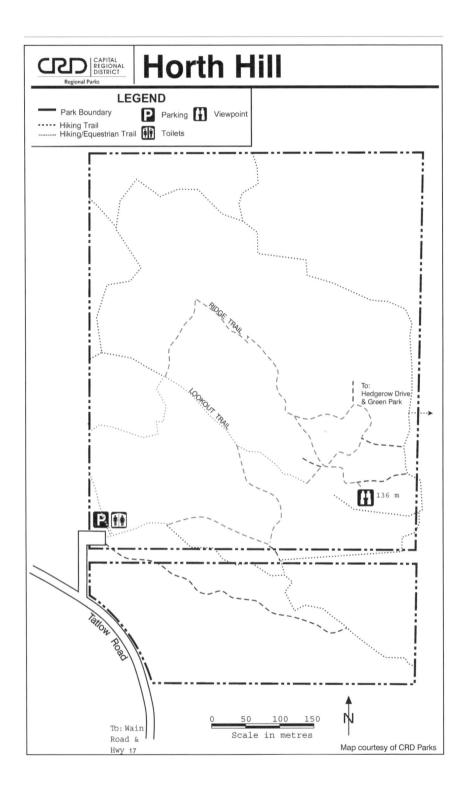

# Horth Hill

## LEGEND

— Park Boundary    **P** Parking    **⌶** Viewpoint
···· Hiking Trail
······ Hiking/Equestrian Trail    **⍆** Toilets

RIDGE TRAIL

LOOKOUT TRAIL

To:
Hedgerow Drive
& Green Park

136 m

**P** **⍆**

Tatlow Road

To: Wain
Road &
Hwy 17

0    50    100    150
Scale in metres

N

Map courtesy of CRD Parks

## 3. Horth Hill

**Highlights:** This (36 ha) CRD regional park in North Saanich features a series of hiking trails that traverse three distinct forest zones. Horth Hill Regional Park created in 1966, has hiking and equestrian trails that meander through park forests. Several trails climb up to a viewpoint near the Horth Hill summit (136 m). Trails are well posted and there is an Information Board.

**Difficulty/Distance:** moderate/30 minutes, one way

**Access:** Follow Highway #17 (Pat Bay) north of Victoria and Sidney, almost to Swartz Bay. At the Wain Road exit turn right onto McDonald Park Road, then right again to take the access across the highway, turn left onto Wain Road and travel west to Tatlow Road. Turn right to the signposted, gated parking lot. Allow around 35 minutes driving time from Victoria. The park is open from sunrise to sunset.

**Hike Description:**

From the main parking lot the northern trail through the forest soon divides. The Ridge Trail is steeper and has loose gravel requiring proper footwear. The Lookout Trail is easier and is often used as a bridle path. You can climb almost to the summit for spectacular vistas of the Saanich Peninsula. The Sunset Bridle Trail loops around base of the hill for an easier walk, which you will share with horse and rider.

As you climb Horth Hill, look for exposed weathered outcrops of Comox Formation sandstone. Horth Hill is a cuesta or hogback hill with its smooth slope to the north and its sharp drop-off to the south. There are other hogback hills on the Saanich Peninsula which also display evidence of glacier grooves. The deep fjord of the Saanich Inlet is testimony to the force of glacial action.

Three forest communities are represented here. First, the heavily shaded western red cedar, then the Douglas-fir/swordfern community at middle elevations. Lastly, near the summit, are the dry, open slopes of the Garry oak landscape. At the viewpoint below the summit a panorama unfolds over the Saanich Peninsula, Satellite Channel and the Gulf Islands.

**Worth Noting:**

- Horth Hill has seasonal wildflowers. Look for the ladyslipper orchid in the spring and mushrooms in the fall.
- Horth Hill is named after a pioneering family who settled the area in 1860.

**Nearby:**

**Green Park** may be reached from a trail that extends east from Horth Hill. Green Park has two man-made ponds and an open meadow, which is seasonally wet.

In this area of North Saanich, there are many hiking and bridle trails connecting parks and ecological reserves. As well, four waterfront parks and a number of beach accesses provide walking enjoyment. Detailed trail maps are available at the Municipality of North Saanich or their website: northsaanich.ca.

Photo: Di Chawner

*On the Trail*

## Hiking is...

- a stress reliever. Hiking is a wonderful escape from the world's busy pace. Troubles disappear as you rest beside a peaceful lake or watch the waves breaking against the shore. As a stress reliever it is hard to beat.

- a physical workout. Looking for a sport that delivers an all around workout while you enjoy the beauty of nature? Hiking is a sport that offers more than just exercise and can be enjoyed by people of all ages.

- affordable. Walking is the easiest, safest and cheapest way to get some exercise. Experts recommend that we should all try to walk briskly for at least a half hour every day.

- a family activity. Hiking can be enjoyed by the whole family. Here is an opportunity to show your children the beauty of the outdoors and teach them to respect and cherish nature. Starting your children hiking is one way to counteract the sedentary lifestyle of TV and video games. Take along a book on wildflowers or birds, and see how many you can identify. Many trails are pet-friendly so include the family dog on a leash.

- a new adventure. Hiking can add new dimensions to your life. It provides opportunities for volunteering with groups to clear stream beds or remove broom or as a volunteer trail warden.

**Confused about kilometres?**
1 metre is 3.3 feet
1 kilometre is .63 miles

# 4. John Dean

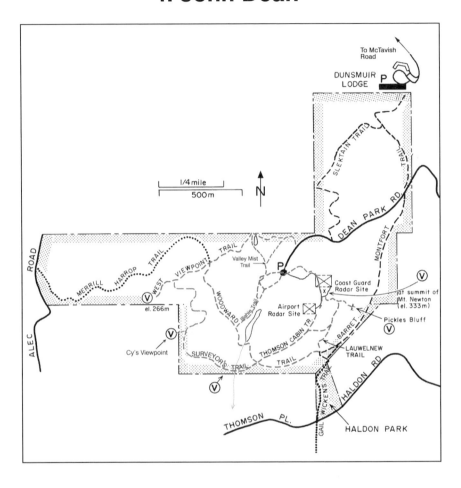

# 4. John Dean

**Highlights:** John Dean Provincial Park, on Mount Newton, harbours one of the Saanich Peninsula's last stands of old-growth Douglas-fir. Numerous hiking trails criss-cross Mount Newton's south and east slopes. There are easy paths through the forest or more strenuous routes that climb to scenic viewpoints. The park's Garry oak hilltops explode with spring wildflowers. No wonder the park is a favourite destination for family day hikes.

**Difficulty/Distance:** easy to moderate/up to 6 km, one way

**Cautions:** Some park trails are steep, narrow and rough. Protruding roots, loose gravel and trailside bushes may impede progress. Other routes are easier and follow old roads or more level terrain. Mossy rock faces are slick in wet weather. Wear proper footwear.

Park trails and side paths are confusing as they are not all marked. Look for trail signposts at key junctions. At Pickles Bluff there are no barricades so stay away from the bluff's sheer edge.

**Access:** From Victoria travel north on Highway #17 (Pat Bay), turn left (west) onto McTavish Road at the traffic light, then left (south) onto East Saanich Road. Continue to Dean Park Road, turn right and follow the park road to the parking area. From Victoria, allow about 35 minutes driving time. There are trail accesses near Dunsmuir Lodge via the Monfort or Slektain trails on the north slope, from Alec Road via the Merrill Harrop Trail (bridle path), and from Thomson Place via the Gail Wickens Trail (bridle path). The park is open from 8 am to sunset. The park road is closed to vehicles from November through March.

Carefully study the park map at the information shelter near the parking area and plot your own hiking route. A popular loop, one that will take you to the West Viewpoint and Pickles Bluff, follows the West Viewpoint, Woodward, Thomson Cabin or Lauwelnew trails. The latter is one of the park's steepest trails. You can shorten your hike around the halfway point by taking the Illahie Trail, near Emerald Pool, back to the parking area. If your hiking route includes the more rugged Surveyor's Trail (which accesses Cy's Viewpoint) be aware there are steep switchbacks to negotiate near Canyon Creek.

**Hike Descriptions:**

**Pickles Bluff:** (moderate/0.5 km, one way) From the parking area hike up the road or the Thunderbird Trail (on the left, parallel to the road) to the federal Department of Transport radar towers. From the viewing platform in a clearing are views over the Gulf Islands. The Mount

Newton summit (306 m) is slightly obscured by the communication towers. Continue east for Pickles Bluff.

Keep left at the Thomson Cabin Trail junction and, after a set of steps, left again at the Lauwelnew Trail junction. The final approach (with more steps) is very steep. Pickles Bluff is a rock outcrop that offers a view southeast of Saanich Peninsula, James Island and the San Juan Islands. There are no barricades so stay away from the bluff's sheer edge.

**Valley Mist Trail:** (easy/0.5 km, one way) Head west from the parking area on a wide path and turn north on the Valley Mist Trail to the beautiful lily pond near the park's northern boundary. In the spring, look for Pacific Coast newts, Pacific tree frogs and pond lilies. The West Viewpoint Trail begins near the dam at the pond's north end. You can loop around the pond and return to the parking area in about 20 minutes.

**West Viewpoint:** (moderate/1 km, one way) Take the Valley Mist Trail to the lily pond and turn west, up the steps, on the West Viewpoint Trail. It is a sharp incline at first then it becomes a more gradual climb and the trail narrows. Watch for roots and loose rocks. Keep straight ahead at the junction where the Woodward and Merrill Harrop trails meet the West Viewpoint Trail. At the end of the trail is a lookout over Finlayson Arm and Brentwood Bay. Allow about an hour (one way) from the parking area.

**Worth Noting:**

- Spring wildflowers in the woods and meadows include shooting stars, camas, trilliums, red paintbrush, sea blush and calypso orchids.
- Mount Newton's forests are a mix of Douglas-fir, western red cedar, grand fir, arbutus and Garry oak.
- Look for Pileated Woodpeckers (Canada's largest) on dead snags. Scan the skies for eagles, Turkey Vultures, hawks and ravens.
- Do not pick any wildflowers.
- The Friends of John Dean Park Association built the major trails through the park. This group is responsible for signage and trail maintenance with the goal of counteracting soil erosion, vegetation destruction and soil compaction. Please stay on marked trails at all times.

**Nearby:**
**Dominion Brook Park** (4.5 ha): Access as for John Dean Park to East Saanich Road. Travel south on East Saanich Road to pass the Panorama Leisure Centre and watch for the park entrance, on the left. Dominion Brook Park has three ponds, a small stream (Dominion Brook), a ravine and sunken garden. There are rare and exotic plant species. Dominion

Brook Park features many heritage trees and shrubs. The park's origins as a federal horticultural demonstration garden date back to 1913. The Friends of Dominion Brook Park, a non-profit society, maintains the park and is working toward its restoration. Park facilities include toilets and a picnic area. Dogs must be leashed.

**Coles Bay Regional Park** (3.6 ha): To reach this CRD park, from Victoria, take Highway #17 (Pat Bay) and then West Saanich Road (#17A) to Ardmore Drive. Turn left here and again on Inverness Road (signposted) to the gated entrance. From Victoria, allow 30 minutes travel time. The park is open from sunrise to sunset. Toilets and picnic facilities near the parking area are wheelchair accessible but the beach and trails are not.

From the parking area follow the Beach or the Nature trails through a mixed forest of Douglas-fir, bigleaf maple and large western red cedar down to Coles Bay, on Saanich Inlet. The hike takes approximately 10 minutes, one way. The rock, pebble and mud beach is best visited at low tide.

In 1921, at the age of 70, John Dean presented 32 ha of his property to the province as parkland. This was the first donated provincial park in BC. Over the years, additional donated lands, including a 7.6 ha parcel given by Sydney Pickles in 1958, have increased the park's size to 174 ha.

During the 1930s federally funded relief crews constructed what we now call Dean Park Road, originally a fire access road, as well as construction of the trails and picnic area in a grove of very large trees. The steps, stone walling and lily pond are still there. This area has been described as "the most beautiful example of dry east coast Douglas-fir old growth in the entire Victoria area."

John Dean passed away in 1943 at the age of 92, having written his own epitaph seven years earlier: "It is a rotten world, artful politicians are its bane. Its saving grace is the artlessness of the young and the wonders of the sky." His grave is in Ross Bay Cemetery beside a large monkey puzzle tree.

# 5. Gowlland Tod

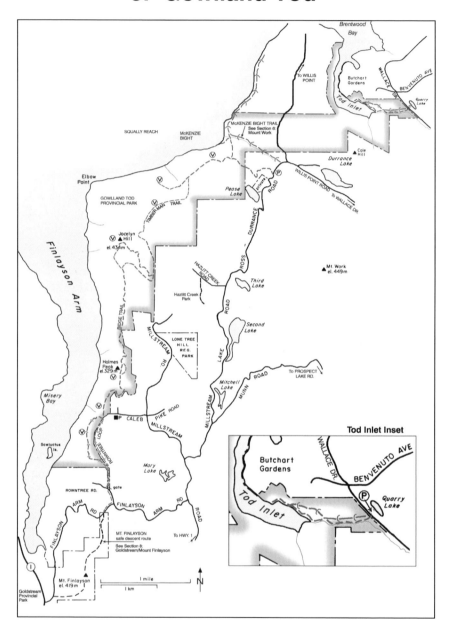

Tod Inlet Inset

# 5. Gowlland Tod

**Highlights:** Gowlland Tod Provincial Park (1200 ha), created in 1995, encompasses picturesque shorelines and forests at Tod Inlet and the rugged 430-m-high Gowlland Range, a series of hills and outcrops that loom above Saanich Inlet's Finlayson Arm, creating the view along the Malahat Drive. This fascinating region, in the Highlands District, has more than 25 km of trails to explore, many of which follow old logging and mining roads to striking viewpoints.

Vibrant wildflowers cover the rocky outcrops through the spring and early summer. The park's forests of Douglas-fir, bigleaf maple, alder, western red cedar and arbutus provide an undisturbed, natural habitat for cougar, black bear, black-tail deer, river otter, mink, red squirrel and other wild animals. There are approximately 100 bird species. The park is a perfect destination for short day hikes or more extended jaunts.

**Difficulty/Distance**: easy to strenuous/1.5 km to 5 km or longer, one way

**Cautions:** Gowlland Tod Park is a wilderness region and the territory of cougar and black bear. Be alert. Keep children close by. Keep all pets leashed. BC Parks recommends you leave your animals at home.

Be prepared for wet, foggy weather. Wear adequate clothing and footwear. Bring rain gear and emergency supplies.

If you are visiting in the wet months, you will encounter mud, slick trails and places where the old roads and trails are flooded into surrounding swampland.

Stay on marked trails to protect the park's rare and fragile ecosystems, particularly around the rocky, open slopes and grassy meadows.

Numerous unmarked trails, confusing old roads and bridle paths criss-cross the area. Respect adjacent private property and do not trespass.

Please ride horses and bikes at a walking pace and only on designated trails (Refer to BC Park maps.)

**Access:** BC Parks has established three park entry points. Hours are sunrise to sunset.

**Wallace Drive (Tod Inlet Access):** From Victoria take Highway #17 (Pat Bay), then West Saanich Road to Wallace Drive and turn left. The trailhead is on the left (west) side of Wallace Drive, opposite Quarry Lake (fenced). There is limited roadside parking. The main trail to Tod Inlet is not wheelchair accessible.

**Ross-Durrance Road (Timberman Trail Access):** From Victoria take Highway #17 (Pat Bay), then West Saanich Road to Wallace Drive and turn left. At Willis Point Road turn left again and continue beyond Durrance Lake to Ross-Durrance Road. Swing left one more time to the parking lot, also on the left. (Mount Work Regional Park hikers share this lot.)

**Caleb Pike Road (Ridge Trail/Mount Finlayson Trail Access):** Follow Highway #1 (Trans-Canada) west from Victoria and take Exit 14 (Langford/Millstream Road). Keep north onto Millstream Road to Caleb Pike Road. Swing left (west) and continue a short distance to the parking lot.

**Hike Descriptions:**

**Tod Inlet:** (moderate/1.5 km, one way): The trail is not wheelchair accessible. There is a choice of routes. From the roadside parking on Wallace Drive, continue past the information kiosk on a wide trail (an old road with a gentle grade) that heads directly to the inlet or turn left and follow the twisting, up-and-down path along Tod Creek. The latter route is worth a visit in the spring, when white fawn lilies and trilliums carpet the forest floor. The rare phantom orchid is much more elusive. The trails end on the idyllic shores of Tod Inlet.

**Timberman Trail to Jocelyn Hill** (strenuous/5 km, one way): From the McKenzie Bight access look for the marked Timberman Trail on Ross-Durrance Road's west side. Soon after you cross Pease Creek is the junction (on the right) with the Cascade Trail, a link to the McKenzie Bight Trail. (See page 44.) Keep left on the Timberman Trail for Jocelyn Hill and, en route, three spectacular viewpoints. The first reveals the wide expanse of Saanich Inlet. At a major junction, keep left for Jocelyn Hill. The path to the right climbs to the Malahat viewpoint and is well worth the side trip. The third viewpoint overlooks Squally Reach. Expect innumerable steep sections and repetitive up-and-down hiking. The trail curves around Jocelyn Hill's southeast slope before veering north on the final pitch to the summit. From here you can extend your hike south to the Caleb Pike parking lot or even further to Mount Finlayson and Goldstream Park.

At the top of Jocelyn Hill (434 m) the breathtaking view takes in the Olympic Mountains, Finlayson Arm, Bamberton, Squally Reach, Saanich Inlet and the Gulf Islands. Watch for Bald Eagles, a variety of hawks (Cooper's, Red-tailed and Sharp-shinned), Peregrine Falcons, ravens and other resident and migrant raptors. You may spot a Golden Eagle or Townsend's Solitaire. More common are Red Crossbills, Cassin's Vireos, Blue Grouse and Merlin. Here and elsewhere in the park's upland forests look for camas, white fawn lilies, larkspur and other spring wildflowers. Jocelyn Hill is known for its April bloom of gold stars.

**Ridge Trail to Jocelyn Hill via Holmes Peak** (strenuous/to Holmes Peak 1.2 km, one way; to Jocelyn Hill 4 km, one way): From the Caleb Pike trailhead, descend behind the information kiosk on the Ridge Trail and keep right at the signposted junction. If you hike the trail in late April or early May look for the delicate ladyslippers and a profusion of shooting stars. Holmes Peak (329 m) offers a fine vista of the Gowlland Range and Finlayson Arm.

Several bridle paths link to the Ridge Trail. Watch for markers to stay on the main trail and ignore any side paths. After a long, arduous climb you will reach upland forest where arbutus, hairy manzanita, and isolated stands of hardy shore pines cling to the exposed rocky outcrops. Follow the markers to the Jocelyn Hill summit. Extend your hike north to the McKenzie Bight access, near Durrance Lake, then stretch your trek even further by adding a hike up Mount Work. (See page 42.)

**Rowntree Loop** (moderate/1.9 km loop): From the Caleb Pike Road trailhead, travel south on the road (an even, steady grade), or descend behind the information kiosk on the signposted Ridge Trail. Be sure to keep left at the fork. The trail drops to several rewarding viewpoints and then climbs again to eventually reach the road, near the park boundary. These are multi-use trails (hiking, cycling and equestrian) so be courteous.

To access the Mount Finlayson Trail continue south on the road and hike between private properties and under power lines to come out on Rowntree Road, near Viart Road. Take Rowntree Road, then turn right (west) on Finlayson Arm Road to the marked Mount Finlayson trailhead, on the left. (See text on page 50; map on page 48.)

**Nearby:**
**Oak Haven Park** (10 ha): Access as for the Tod Inlet trailhead. Parking is limited at both locations. Continue north on Wallace Drive to Benvenuto Avenue and turn right (east) to the park. This municipal park features large Douglas-fir, arbutus and Garry oak. Among the rock outcrops look for Indian plum and Nootka Rose and other flowering shrubs. Wildflowers include trillium, camas, satin flowers and fawn lilies.

**Gore Park:** To reach pretty and unspoiled Gore Park, from Benvenuto Avenue keep north on Wallace Drive to Greig Avenue and turn right (east) to the park. The spring wildflowers here are a delight.

**Trails** at Lone Tree Hill, Mount Work, Durrance Lake and Goldstream Park (via Mount Finlayson) are close by. (See pages 42, 46 and 48.)

The Saanich Inlet is significant in being the only deep water fjord on Vancouver Island's east coast and one of only four "shallow sill" fjords in the world. A very deep basin hemmed in by a shallow outlet, the inlet experiences little tidal flushing, creating a unique marine ecosystem including a bottom layer devoid of oxygen. Finlayson Arm's diverse marine life includes boot and cloud sponges, wolf eels and lamp shells.

In February of 2006, scientists and researchers from the University of Victoria began operating the 10.3 million dollar VENUS project (Victoria Experimental Network Under The Sea), which is an underwater observatory designed to retrieve data from the Saanich Inlet seabed. The specialized equipment retrieves continuous streams of data collected by underwater sensors and transmits it to computers, where it is processed by UVIC's data management systems. The information is then posted on their web site for use anywhere in the world. This equipment allows scientists to study and monitor changing conditions on the seabed. VENUS is expected to revolutionize the study of ocean science.

~ ~ ~

Wallace Drive, the main approach to the beautiful Tod Inlet trails, follows the old railbed of the BC Electric Railway, built to serve Tod Inlet and Deep Cove. Tod Inlet was the location of the townsite and cement works of the Vancouver Portland Cement Company (1904-1920s) where about 400 people lived and worked. It is adjacent to Butchart Gardens (you can hear the fountain from area trails) created by Jenny Butchart from worked-out limestone quarries.

~ ~ ~

The First Nations people called Tod Inlet "the place of the blue grouse." Tod Inlet is named after John Tod, who first arrived in British Columbia in 1823. In 1850, after a long career with Hudson's Bay Company, he became the first person ever to retire in Victoria. Tod served on the Council of Government for the colony of Vancouver Island and later on the legislative council. Mary Tod Islet, just offshore in Oak Bay, is named after John Tod's second daughter.

The Gowlland Range is named for John Thomas Gowlland, RN, a coastal surveyor who served as second master under Captain Richards aboard HMS *Plumper* (1857-1860) and HMS *Hecate* (1861-1863).

**Map and Compass**
While most of the hikes in this book do not require navigation by map and compass, this skill is a necessity if you are to hike in some of the larger backcountry areas beyond Victoria, such as East Sooke or Gowlland Tod parks, which offer a good variety of trails to test your competence. A map and compass are essential if you should choose to go cross-country between trails, something which is not generally recommended, certainly not without these tools. It is amazing how quickly one can become turned around and lost.

Maps are available from many park organizations and municipalities and may provide more detailed information than is found in the maps in this book. It is recommended that these be acquired if any of the more difficult areas are visited. Because topographical maps show the shape of the land, they are the most suitable type of map for most outdoor activities. They show the topography or shape of the land in addition to other features such as roads, rivers, lakes, etc.

A compass is used for orienting maps to the terrain and often for simply deciding on direction of travel. Compasses are available at a variety of prices and some may be pre-adjusted for the difference between true and magnetic north.

For those who want further challenges the sport of orienteering has many adherents, including members of the VictOrienteers Club (see orienteeringbc.ca/vico) and is one way to learn how to use map and compass successfully. Orienteering involves cross-country navigation by foot over unknown terrain, using a map and a compass. It can be relaxing, or challenging and competitive. The club offers courses of varying degrees of difficulty.

Global Positioning System, or GPS, devices are wonderful instruments. They are great fun and useful tools. But be careful! Do not rely on a GPS until you first prepare yourself with the knowledge and skills required to find your way with a map and compass.

# 6. Mount Work

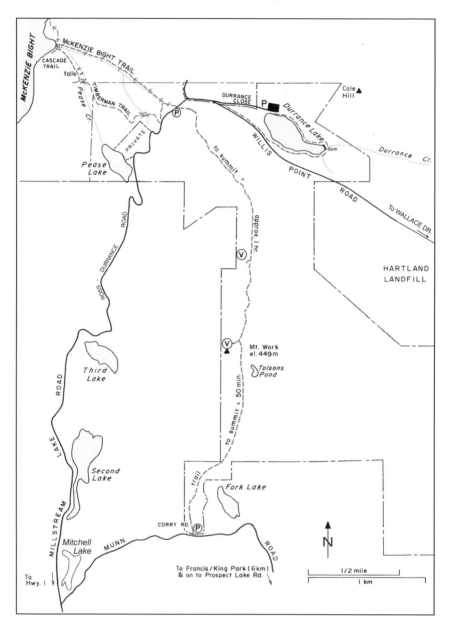

# 6. Mount Work

**Highlights:** Mount Work Park, in the Highlands District, has 11 km of captivating trails through upland and lowland forests. The steep climb to the Mount Work summit is somewhat challenging but hikers are treated to a striking view of southern Vancouver Island from the highest point on the Saanich Peninsula. Mount Work Regional Park (577 ha), among the largest in the CRD system, has three lakes. Durrance Lake, the most accessible, has an attractive loop trail. One trail descends to Saanich Inlet.

**Difficulty/Distance:** moderate to strenuous/1.7 km to 2.5 km, one way

**Cautions:** Both Mount Work routes are fairly steep in parts and there are several switchbacks. The open rock faces near the summit may be extremely slippery in wet weather.

Storms and fog may roll in without warning. Gear up for potentially adverse conditions and wear proper footwear.

**Access:**
**To the Main Entrance (north end trailhead):** From Victoria take Highway #17 (Pat Bay), then West Saanich Road to Wallace Drive and turn left. At Willis Point Road turn left again and continue to Ross-Durrance Road. Swing left one more time to the parking lot, also on the left. (Gowlland Tod Provincial Park hikers park here too.)

**For Durrance Lake:** Follow directions as above to Willis Point Road. Turn right at Durrance Close, which leads to the parking lot.

**For the Fork Lake Entrance (south end trailhead):** From Victoria, take Highway #1 (Trans-Canada) and cut off at Helmcken Road interchange (Exit 8). Head north to Burnside Road West and turn left. Continue to Prospect Lake Road and turn right. Near Francis King Park, make a left on Munn Road, and wind another 6 km through the Highlands to the park entrance and tiny parking area on the right, just past Fork Lake Road.

From Victoria, allow about 40 minutes driving time. The park is open from sunrise to sunset. The north side of Durrance Lake is wheelchair-accessible.

**Hike Descriptions:**
**Summit Trail** (strenuous/from north trailhead, 2.5 km, one way; from south trailhead, 1.8 km, one way): The rugged Summit Trail stretches north to south, from one end of the park to the other. You have a choice of starting points, but the distance to the top is a little shorter from the Fork Lake trailhead than from the one near Durrance Lake. (Note:

Whichever trailhead you choose and just after you begin hiking, swing right at the first junction for the summit.)

The cool, moist, lowland forest consists of mainly maple, western red cedar, alder and Douglas-fir. The drier uplands have Douglas-fir, lodgepole pine and arbutus. There are open areas and beautiful views on the way up that include Central Saanich and the Haro Strait islands. At the top of Mount Work (449 m) the spectacular summit viewpoint takes in Victoria, Lone Tree Hill, Finlayson Arm, the Malahat, Jocelyn Hill, Juan de Fuca Strait and the Olympic Mountains.

**Durrance Lake Trail** (moderate/1.7 km, one way): Hemmed in by Mount Work and the Partridge Hills, Durrance Lake (8.4 ha) is a popular hiking, swimming and fishing destination. From the parking lot the Durrance Lake Trail leads to the lake's east end, close to a dam on Durrance Creek. From here the groomed path narrows considerably and loops back along the lake's south side. The trail follows a serpentine course as it meanders through the damp, boggy lowland forest and eventually emerges on Durrance Close, near the parking lot.

**McKenzie Bight Trail** (moderate/1.5 km, one way): This pleasant hike traverses a multi-use trail (hiking, biking and equestrians) and starts from the shared parking lot on Ross-Durrance Road. Cross over to the road's west side and follow the signposted McKenzie Bight Trail. It is a steady drop most of the way and the return climb will take you slightly longer than your descent. The shady forest floor alongside McKenzie Creek is covered with mosses, lichen and ferns of many types. The ferns are exceptionally thick in the ravine (the grotto), near a fine stand of western red cedar and Douglas-fir. In early April, the Rufous Hummingbird is a common sight.

The trail emerges at McKenzie Bight, close to Squally Reach. There are waterside picnic spots. Take time to examine the diversity of seaweed that flourishes in the estuary near the mud, sand and pebble beach. Harbour seals are sometimes observed offshore. A 21-m-wide parkland strip extends northeast from McKenzie Bight along a rough road to the end of Mark Lane. To loop hike back, cross the McKenzie Creek bridge and follow the Cascade and Timberman trails to the start. The Cascade Trail (moderate 0.5 km), on McKenzie Creek's west side, passes several clamorous waterfalls and a viewpoint on Pease Creek.

**Worth Noting:**

- Wildflowers to look for include fawn lilies, trilliums, shooting stars and Indian paintbrush. Shrubs like Oregon grape and oceanspray are common.

- The shrub at Mount Work's summit that resembles an arbutus tree is actually hairy manzanita, a close relative. The clusters of white or pink flowers turn into dark berries in the fall.

- From the Mount Work summit, watch for Turkey Vultures high in the thermals. In the late summer, these large birds congregate here, in small flocks. Their fall migration south begins with a crossing of Juan de Fuca Strait. Other birds of prey to watch for are hawks and Bald Eagles.

- Ferns and salmonberries thrive along parts of the Durrance Lake Trail. Look for banana slugs underfoot and western red-backed salamanders near decaying trees.

- You can hike in the Mount Work area any month of the year, barring times of snow at higher elevations. The summit trails are exposed to the weather.

- Please keep to the main trails at all times to protect fragile vegetation.

- Toilets are located at Durrance Lake and near the parking area on Ross-Durrance Road.

- Please stay off surrounding private property.

**Nearby:**
**The Mount Work-Hartland mountain bike trails** on Mount Work's east slope are also part of the park. The trails here are multi-use, cycling, hiking, and horseback riding. Contact the South Island Mountain Bike Society (SIMBS) for access and permit information at: simbs.com.

**Gowlland Tod Provincial Park** abuts Mount Work Park. From the shared Ross-Durrance Road parking lot, a hiking-only trail leads to several viewpoints, Jocelyn Hill and beyond. (See page 36.)

Mount Work is a monadnock, or residual hill, whose hard rock (Wark gneiss) survived the grinding action of scouring glaciers. Evidence of their passing is all around this area. A little to the west lies Finlayson Arm, a glacial fjord. Along the McKenzie Bight Trail look for deposits of layered gravel and clay.

# 7. Lone Tree Hill

Photo: Joyce Folbigg

**Highlights:** The small (32 ha), Lone Tree Hill Regional Park is located in the Highlands District. The park offers excellent viewpoints, fine examples of dry, rocky outcrop vegetation and birdwatching opportunities.

**Difficulty/Distance:** moderate to strenuous/1.2 km, one way

**Cautions:** Avoid the open slopes near the summit.

**Access:**
From Victoria, take Highway #1 (Trans-Canada), leave the highway at Exit 14 and follow the right hand lane onto Millstream Road. Stay on this road, travelling north and at the junction of Millstream Road and Millstream Lake Road, bear left. Millstream Road is signed as a "no through road" at this point. The park is on the right side of the road about 1.5 kilometres beyond Caleb Pike Road.

**Hike Description:**
From the parking area the steep, rocky trail climbs steadily for 1.2 km to the summit (364 m). At the top there are spectacular views of the Malahat, the Gowlland Range, Victoria and the Olympic Mountains. Stay on the trail to protect the area's delicate ecology.

**Worth Noting:**

- The park is a popular birdwatching destination. Soaring Turkey Vultures, Red-tailed Hawks and eagles may be seen riding overhead thermals.

- Wildflowers (shooting stars, camas, fairy orchids, sea blush, sedum and fawn lilies) are abundant in the spring, particularly near the summit.

- The park created in 1982, was named after a solitary, bonsai-like Douglas-fir tree that stood on the summit for over 200 years.

# 8. Goldstream/Mount Finlayson

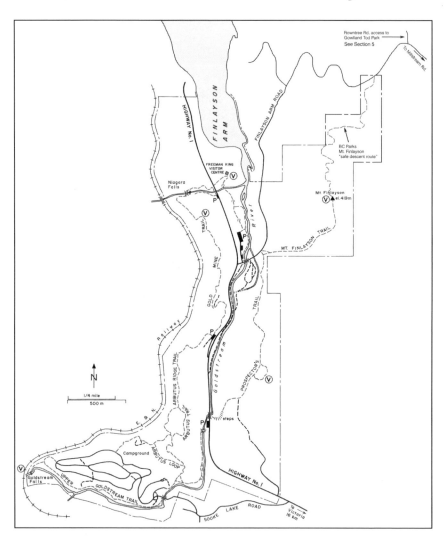

## 8. Goldstream/Mount Finlayson

**Highlights:** Goldstream Provincial Park (388 ha) features almost 16 km of year round hiking trails through forested uplands and lowlands, each with their own characteristics. The park has 600-year-old Douglas-fir, large western red cedar, arbutus and Garry oak. There are superb opportunities for wildlife viewing and nature appreciation. The fall chum salmon run draws thousands of visitors. The Freeman King Visitor Centre near the Goldstream River estuary has seasonal interpretive programs.

**Difficulty/Distance:** easy to strenuous/15 minutes to 1.5 hours or more, one way

**Cautions:** Use extreme caution if crossing Highway #1.

Be careful as bicycles are allowed on the trail from the parking lot to the Visitor Centre.

The Mount Finlayson Trail is well known for accidents. It is not recommended for pets or small children. Please take this mountain seriously.

Parts of Goldstream Park are semi-wilderness regions and the territory of cougar and black bear. Be alert. Keep children close by.

Avoid the treacherous steep slopes in the Niagara Canyon on the Gold Mine Trail.

**Access:** Take Highway #1 (Trans-Canada) about 30 minutes (16 km) west of Victoria to Goldstream Park's southern boundary, where you will see a portal sign. Keep straight ahead on Highway #1 and drop down the hill to the day-use/picnic area and pay parking lot, near the junction of the highway and Finlayson Arm Road. There are three day-use parking lots on the southbound lane of the highway. The more northerly one serves the Niagara Falls viewpoint.

**Freeman King Visitor Centre:** A short trail extends from the day use/picnic area to the Freeman King Visitor Centre. Here you will find historical displays and a viewing platform close to the Goldstream River estuary and salt marsh. This is an excellent spot to watch for deer, mink, river otters, eagles, migrating hummingbirds (March) and various shorebirds and ducks (late spring/early summer). Please observe the estuary's quiet zone regulations. Several short trails starting from the day-use parking lot are wheelchair accessible.

Goldstream Provincial Park has a full-service 173-site campground. Interpretive programs offered by the Visitor Centre during the spawning chum salmon run (usually late October to early December) or the "Eagle

Extravaganza" (December to February) are extremely popular. Contact BC Parks for times and details, and for information on fees, reservations and additional trails. (See page 167.)

**Hike Descriptions:**
As well as the hikes listed below there are several short, interconnecting trails along the river, close to the day-use/picnic area. Many trails have good viewpoints and some join other paths making it easy to create your own loop hike.

**Arbutus Trail** (easy/15 minutes, one way) and the **Arbutus Ridge** (moderate/1.5 hours, one way) pass through stands of arbutus trees and Garry oak that prefer drier upland areas. The spring season brings a profusion of wildflowers.

**Lower Goldstream Trail** (easy/15 minutes, one way) winds along the Goldstream River and is a great spot to view the fall chum salmon run. Chinook and coho salmon also enter the river. Watch for river otter, mink and American dippers.

**Upper Goldstream Trail**, near the campsite, (easy/1/2 hour, one way) is the trail to hike if you like big trees. Highlights include some of the park's oldest trees and 8-m-high Goldstream Falls.

**Gold Mine Trail** (moderate/1 hour, one way) climbs to the top of 47.5 m-high Niagara Falls on Niagara Creek. A footbridge spans the Niagara Canyon. Avoid the treacherous steep slopes in this area. The route passes old mine workings and a spring. A short trail accesses the bottom of Niagara Falls. Use extreme caution when crossing Highway #1.

**Prospector's Trail** (moderate/1.5 hours, one way) links the campsite with the Mount Finlayson Trail. You will see large Douglas-fir, Garry oak and arbutus. There is a great viewpoint and old copper mine workings.

**Mount Finlayson Trail** (strenuous/1 hour, plus, one way) begins on the east side of the Goldstream River bridge (close to the day use/picnic area) and accesses one of Victoria's best viewpoints. Be prepared for adverse and changeable weather conditions on the challenging and steady (almost 2 km) climb to the summit (419 m). Wear adequate clothing and footwear. Beware of exposed, steep drop-offs and bluffs. Some rock scrambling is required. Watch for orange markings on rocks that indicate the route. Sections of trail may be extremely slippery when wet. Allow adequate time during daylight hours for your return hike.

To descend from the summit, it is recommended that hikers use the "safe" route that snakes down the north flank of Mount Finlayson to Finlayson

Arm Road. The trail is 4 km long. At the bottom, follow the trail links to Gowlland Tod Provincial Park (See map on page 36.) or circle back to the Goldstream Park parking lot via Finlayson Arm Road. Use caution on this narrow road. There is no sidewalk.

**Worth Noting:**

- Stay on marked trails to protect the park's rare and fragile ecosystems.
- Bicycles are allowed only on the trail from the parking lot to the Visitor Centre.

**Nearby:**
**Gowlland Tod Provincial Park trails** may be accessed from Finlayson Arm Road. (See page 36.)

---

The Goldstream area is a traditional First Nations fishing ground and the site of a mid-1800s gold rush. In 1958, the Greater Victoria Water Board donated the land at Goldstream Park to the province. Later additions were acquired in 1994 through the Commonwealth Nature Legacy Program.

~ ~ ~

The Outdoor Club of Victoria constructed the Arbutus Ridge, Gold Mine, Prospector's and Riverside trails. The club designed the stairs and CRD have adopted that plan for building other trail stairs.

---

**Bicycles**
Bicycles are not permitted on hiking trails. Multi-use trails are indicated in the text. See Legend, page 10 to identify trails on the maps.

# 9. Francis/King

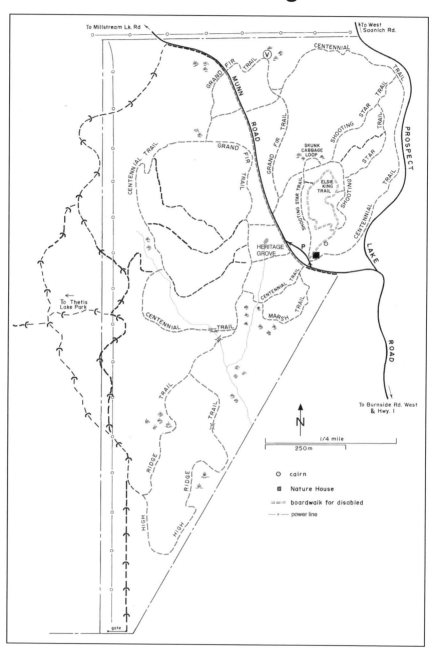

To Millstream Lk. Rd

To West
Saanich Rd.

CENTENNIAL

GRAND FIR TRAIL

MUNN ROAD

GRAND FIR TRAIL

GRAND FIR TRAIL

CENTENNIAL TRAIL

SHOOTING STAR TRAIL

SKUNK
CABBAGE
LOOP

ELSIE
KING
TRAIL

SHOOTING STAR TRAIL

SHOOTING STAR

PROSPECT

HERITAGE
GROVE

P

LAKE

To Thetis
Lake Park

CENTENNIAL TRAIL

CENTENNIAL TRAIL

MARSH TRAIL

ROAD

To Burnside Rd. West
& Hwy. 1

N

1/4 mile
250 m

RIDGE TRAIL

RIDGE

HIGH

HIGH

TRAIL

○   cairn

▣   Nature House

===   boardwalk for disabled

— ○ —   power line

gate

# 9. Francis/King

**Highlights:** There are approximately 11 km of year-round hiking trails at the CRD's Francis/King Regional Park (109 ha). The paths, well-sign-posted and groomed, are perfect for family outings. The Elsie King Interpretive Trail is specially designed for wheelchair accessibility. The park has bigleaf maple, red alder, western flowering dogwood, towering western red cedars, grand fir and some of Saanich's tallest and oldest old-growth Douglas-fir. Splashes of spring wildflowers carpet the forest floor. The Nature House features displays of the park's flora and fauna and offers interpretive programs.

**Difficulty/Distance:** easy to moderate/up to 2.8 km, or longer, one way

**Cautions:** Some park trails have slight elevation changes with moderate grades. Rock outcrops and boardwalks may be slippery in wet weather. There are muddy sections and exposed roots so tread carefully and wear proper footgear.

**Access:** From Victoria, take Highway #1 (Trans-Canada) and cut off at the Helmcken Road interchange (Exit 8). Head north to Burnside Road West and turn left. Continue to Prospect Lake Road and turn right. One kilometre along swing left on Munn Road. The parking lot is just ahead, on the right. From Victoria, allow 20 minutes driving time. The park is open 8 am to 9 pm (April to October)/8 am to 5 pm (October to April). The Elsie King Trail, toilets and Nature House are wheelchair accessible. For information on the Nature House hours and interpretive programs offered, contact CRD Parks. (See page 167.)

**Hike Descriptions:**

**Elsie King Interpretive Trail** (easy/750 m loop): Starting near the Nature House, this self-guiding interpretive trail is wheel-chair-friendly. It consists of hard-packed gravel and cedar boardwalks that cross sensitive areas. There are benches and rest areas, interpretive signposts and a shelter. The trail through stately Douglas-fir and grand fir is great for hikers of all ages. NO dogs on this trail.

**Access to Heritage Grove** (easy/200 m, one way): The park's Heritage Grove features 500-year-old Douglas-fir up to 3 m in circumference and 75 m tall. From the parking lot, cross Munn Road to the west side. Turn right at the fence gate and follow the bridle path north, along Munn Road, to a second fence gate. Turn left and go through. The largest diameter Douglas-fir (3 m) is on the right, just before the creek.

Continue down a steep grade and cross the creek. Near the Grand Fir Trail junction, look for the tallest Douglas-fir (75 m), estimated at 500 years old.

Some trees here bear the scars of a forest fire that surged through the area in the 1950s. To extend your hike, bear left (south) to the Centennial Trail junction and return via that route, with the 15-minute Marsh Trail as an added option, or simply retrace your steps.

**High Ridge Trail** (moderate/2.8 km, one way): From the parking lot cross Munn Road to the west side and go through the fence gate onto the Centennial Trail and down a hill. At the first junction, swing left for a side trip onto the Marsh Trail, a 0.6-km loop (15 minutes) through area lowlands. A profusion of swamp lantern (skunk cabbage) is evident in the spring. Alder and Indian plum are also abundant. Watch for protruding roots and expect muddy sections.

Back on the Centennial Trail continue straight ahead to cross another stream. The trail starts a climb to the ridge. At the next signpost where the Centennial Trail swings off to the right, keep left onto the High Ridge Trail. At the next fork you can go either way since the ridge trail circles back to this point. Expect some up and down stretches with moderate grades. You will pass rock outcrops (look for glacial scouring marks), open areas and some southeast views. Avoid the trail that runs west to connect with Thetis Lake. Backtrack to the Centennial Trail and out to the parking lot.

Other trail options (about 30 minutes) include the Grand Fir and Shooting Star trails (both are 1.3 km in length and link to the Centennial Trail) or the longer (1 hour) Centennial Trail (2.7 km) that loops around the park.

**Worth Noting:**

- The park features spring wildflowers (including shooting stars, spring gold, white fawn lilies and camas), ferns, lichens and mosses. In the fall various types of fungi appear.
- Some park bird species to look for are woodpeckers (Pileated, Hairy and Downy), Steller's Jays, Winter Wrens, chickadees, Cedar Waxwings and warblers. Hawks and Turkey Vultures may be visible overhead.
- Red squirrels, the introduced gray squirrel, bats, snakes, black-tailed deer, and raccoons all live in the park. Hard-to-spot Pacific tree frogs may be heard near swampy bottomlands.
- In the drier uplands, where arbutus and Garry oak dominate the hilltops, you'll find oceanspray, salal and snowberry.
- A bridle path parallels Munn Road and cuts through the park.

**Nearby:**
Multi-use trails (hiking, biking and equestrian) link Francis/King Park with Thetis Lake. These routes run generally north/south along Francis/King Park's western boundary and may be accessed from Munn Road, the Centennial Trail or the High Ridge Trail. You can also hike from Thetis Lake to Mill Hill. (See pages 86 and 90.)

Francis/King Park consists of two properties, one on each side of Munn Road. The eastern sector was donated to the province in 1960 by Thomas Francis and became Thomas Francis Park. The land on the west side was transferred from the City of Victoria to the province in 1967 and became Freeman King Park. Freeman King was a well-known naturalist, conservationist and Boy Scout leader. The Elsie King Trail is named after his wife, a well-liked leader of Victoria's Girl Guides. At one time the Victoria Natural History Society looked after both parks.

# 10. Elk/Beaver Lake

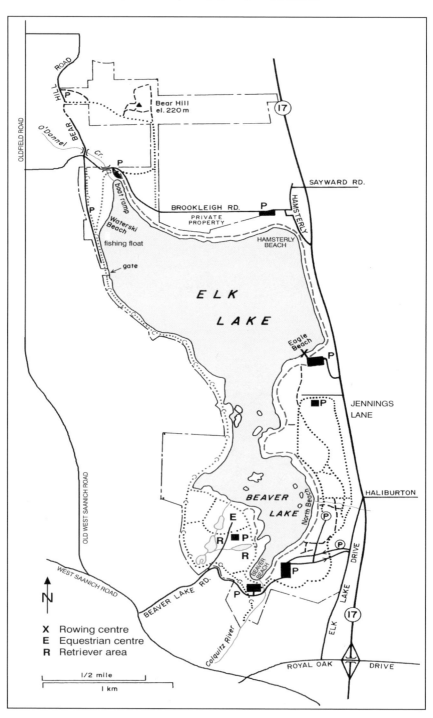

Bear Hill
el. 220 m

17

SAYWARD RD.

BROOKLEIGH RD.    P

PRIVATE
PROPERTY

HAMSTERLY
BEACH

boat ramp

Waterski
Beach

fishing float

gate

E L K

L A K E

Eagle
Beach
X    P

P    JENNINGS
LANE

HALIBURTON

BEAVER

LAKE

E

R  P

R

P

P

P

N

X  Rowing centre
E  Equestrian centre
R  Retriever area

1/2 mile

1 km

OLDFIELD ROAD

OLD WEST SAANICH ROAD

WEST SAANICH ROAD

BEAVER LAKE RD.

Colquitz River

ELK LAKE DRIVE

ROYAL OAK    DRIVE

17

56

## 10. Elk/Beaver Lake

**Highlights:** The CRD's Elk/Beaver Lake Regional Park (443 ha) in Saanich sees close to a million visitors a year. It's a multi-use park enjoyed by hikers, equestrians, cyclists, swimmers, paddlers, rowers, fishers, windsurfers, boaters and dog trainers. A 10-km trail loops around both lakes and there are plenty of shorter paths to explore. Elk Lake is the largest lake in the area.

**Difficulty/Distance:** easy/up to 10 km loop

**Cautions:** Cyclists and equestrians are allowed on the 10K Trail, but only the section that runs along the west side of the lakes.

**Access to Elk Lake:** From Victoria, take Highway #17 (Pat Bay) north past Elk Lake to Sayward Road and turn left at the traffic lights. Make a second left onto Hamsterly Road and a right onto Brookleigh Road to the park entrance at Hamsterly Beach. Parking is also available at Brookleigh Boat Launch, Waterski Beach and the fishing float on Elk Lake's west side (disabled parking only). Check with CRD parks for seasonal restrictions and closures. (See page 167.)

**To Beaver Lake:** From Victoria, take Highway #17 (Pat Bay) north, then take the Royal Oak exit and turn left on Royal Oak Drive. Cross the highway overpass and follow Royal Oak Drive to Elk Lake Drive. Turn right at the lights and continue to the park entrance, up ahead on the left. There are several parking lots including North Beach, Beaver Beach and the one next to the old filter beds at the lake's southern tip.

From Victoria, allow around 20 minutes driving time. The park is open from sunrise to sunset. Beaver Beach, the 10K Trail, some shorter paths, Hamsterly Beach, Brookleigh Boat Launch and the Elk Lake fishing float are wheelchair accessible.

**Hike Description:**

**The 10K Trail** circles Beaver Lake and Elk Lake (224 ha combined size) and winds through forests, fields and wetlands. There are stands of crabapple, western red cedar, cottonwood, Pacific willow, bigleaf maple and alder. The trail has many access points along the way. Start at Beaver Beach, at Beaver Lake's south end, turn left and cross the Colquitz Creek footbridge. Stay on the trail closest to the lake. Paths on the left lead to the park's Equestrian Centre and the dog training area at the retriever ponds. Contact local clubs concerning access.

The 10K Trail heads north to follow the relatively flat railbed of the defunct Victoria and Sidney (V & S) Railroad. This section is shared with equestrians and cyclists. The trail passes a fishing platform and heads north alongside Bear Hill Road (south end) to Waterski Beach and the Brookleigh boat launch. Here the route turns east to skirt Elk Lake's north shore to Hamsterly Beach.

Continue south, where the trail narrows and becomes uneven, to parallel Pat Bay Highway. Eagle Beach, close to the Victoria Rowing Society boathouse and dock, is a favourite swimming area. At this point the trail branches, with one path keeping close to Elk Lake and the other running alongside an open, grassy field. Look for cascara trees in this area. Dogs are often trained here where they are allowed off-leash. Both trails lead back to Beaver Beach and the parking lot. You can shorten your 10K Trail hike by half a kilometre by keeping to the lakeside paths.

**Worth Noting:**

- The lakes are home to painted turtles, frogs, river otters, mink, Canada Geese, mergansers, kingfishers, buffleheads and other waterfowl.
- The City of Victoria created Elk/Beaver Lake Park in 1923; in 1966 it became a regional park.

**Nearby:**

**Bear Hill Regional Park** (49 ha) is accessed as for Elk Lake to Brookleigh Road. Stay on Brookleigh Road and turn right on Oldfield Road. Swing right onto Bear Hill Road (north end) to the main park entrance. You can also reach this point on foot via the right-of-way that links to the southern part of Bear Hill Road or the hiking/bridle trail off Brookleigh Road just before the boat launch. There are a number of bridle trails shared with hikers. This CRD park has no facilities and is not wheelchair accessible.

**Bear Hill summit trail** (moderate/1 km, one way) is steep, with loose gravel in some sections. Open rock faces become extremely slippery in wet weather. On your hike, notice how the forest changes from Douglas-fir to arbutus, then to dry, open grassy areas and Garry oak meadows. Be sure to climb every knoll and false summit in order to catch every one of the many views. The best is at the Bear Hill summit (220 m). The panorama of the Gulf Islands, Haro Strait, Saanich Peninsula and Sidney is definitely worth the climb.

**Bear Hill's spring wildflowers** include satin flowers (in March) followed by blue camas, fawn lilies, sea-blush and canary violet. Please do not pick any flowers. The park's denser woodlands are good places to look for the Varied Thrush or Towhee. Listen for the telltale thrum of hidden grouse.

In 1872 the Colquitz River was dammed across a natural outlet, raising the water level to form a single lake, creating Victoria's first domestic water reservoir. Filter beds were constructed in 1896 at Beaver Lake's south end. Victoria residents were complaining that tadpoles and fish were flowing from household taps. When Victoria changed to Sooke for its water supply in 1914, the filter beds were abandoned.

~ ~ ~

On Beaver Lake's west side the trail follows the bed of the old Victoria and Sidney Railroad. Opened in 1894, the rail route ran from Victoria through Royal Oak, Keating and Saanichton. In its peak year, 1913, it carried 123,599 passengers and 45,282 tonnes of freight. Steam-driven and fired by wood, the V & S was nicknamed the "Cordwood Limited".

~ ~ ~

Bear Hill (like Mount Work, Mount Douglas and Mount Tolmie) is a monadock, a residual hill left behind by receding glaciers about 15,000 years ago. Here the ice was about 1000 metres thick. Striations (grooves and scratches on area rocks) are evidence of their passing.

~ ~ ~

The Victoria Rowing Society boathouse is located near Eagle Beach, on Elk Lake's southeast corner. Built in 1986, the boathouse is an Olympic Rowing Centre used by rowers from the Canadian National Team, the Victoria Rowing Society, the Greater Victoria Youth Rowing Society and the University of Victoria. Elk Lake is an exceptional year round training setting.

# 11. Rithet's Bog

Photo: Aldyth Hunter

Rithet's Bog was donated to Saanich in 1994 by the Guinness family of Britain, the brewers of Guinness stout. The Guinness cairn, located near the corner of Chatterton Way and Dalewood Lane, marks their generosity. The bog is named after Robert Patterson Rithet. In 1889, the wealthy businessman and one-time Victoria mayor who built the Ogden Point wharves bought land in the area and called it Broadmead Farm, after a favourite stallion.

## 11. Rithet's Bog

**Highlights:** Saanich's Rithet's Bog Conservation Area preserves the last of Greater Victoria's sphagnum bogs. Located in Broadmead, the area is excellent for birdwatching. A meandering trail circles the marshland.

**Difficulty/Distance:** easy, 3 km loop

**Cautions:** Stay on the trail at all times. The sphagnum bog conceals dangerous areas of deep water.

Do not forget to bring insect repellent during mosquito season.

**Access:** From Victoria, follow Highway #17 (Pat Bay) north and take the Quadra Street Exit, turn right on Quadra Street, then left onto Chatterton Way. Continue about 1 km to Dalewood Lane and a small parking area across from the houses on the street's south side.

A bicycle rack is available by the Information Board. Sections of the trail cross uneven ground where visitors in wheelchairs will require assistance.

**Hike Description:**

The 3-km perimeter trail circles Rithet's Bog (38.4 ha). The relatively flat trail is hard-packed gravel and chip bark. The southeast side has some moderate inclines. You will see interpretive signs and benches en route. A viewing platform is located on Dalewood Lane. Around the marshland are bulrushes, cattails, willows and scattered patches of shore pine, arbutus, aspen or cottonwood. On drier ground, arbutus, Douglas-fir and Garry oak dominate. This varied habitat makes Rithet's Bog a prime birdwatching destination. It's also a great spot to observe seasonal butterflies including the rare ringlet butterfly.

**Worth Noting:**

- Part of the perimeter trail follows Fir Tree Glen.
- Cyclists are not permitted on the trail.

**Nearby:**
**The Rolston Trail**, near the Gabo Creek bridge, runs east through Shadywood and Emily Carr parks to link with other Broadmead area trails and urban walks. You can connect to the Lochside Trail via Grant or Donwood parks. The trail is named to honour Gordon A. Rolston, a Broadmead community planner. Through his efforts in the 1960s, many natural areas were preserved as linear green spaces and now make up part of the Broadmead trail network.

# 12. Mount Douglas

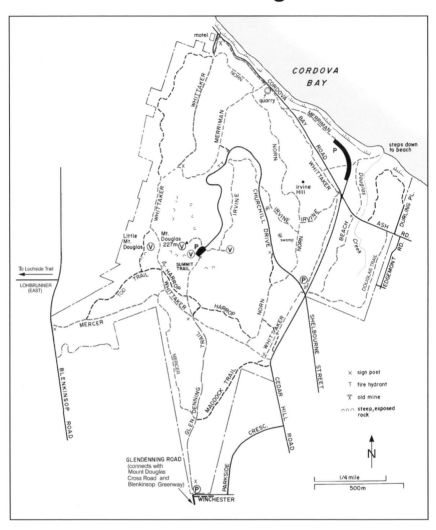

# 12. Mount Douglas

**Highlights:** Mount Douglas Park (181.5 ha), in Gordon Head, is Saanich's largest park. Interconnecting trails, of varying degrees of difficulty, lead hikers to sandy ocean beaches, down shady, fern-lined paths within Douglas-fir and western red cedar forests, and on more challenging routes that climb to Garry oak hilltop viewpoints. The park's spring wildflowers are a delight and the birdwatching unequalled. The 360-degree panorama at the Mount Douglas summit is one of southern Vancouver Island's best and one of Victoria's most popular year-round destinations.

**Difficulty/Distance:** easy to strenuous/200 m to 3.8 km and up, one way

**Cautions:** Signage is incomplete at many trail junctions. Carry accurate maps.

**Access**: Mount Douglas Park has several designated parking areas. Trails may also be reached from numerous points around the park's perimeter. There are marked trailheads along Cordova Bay Road from which you can plan some good hiking. No parking is allowed on Cordova Bay Road. From downtown Victoria, allow 20 minutes driving time. Contact Saanich Parks for horse restrictions and seasonal dog regulations. (See page 167.)

**Main Parking Lot:** From Victoria, travel north on Shelbourne Street, to the intersection of Cordova Bay and Ash roads. Drive straight ahead and to the right to the main parking lot. Washrooms (wheelchair accessible), a children's playground and picnic areas are close by. A short path (200 m) and a set of steps lead from the parking area down to Cordova Bay and the sandy beach.

**Churchill Road:** A tiny roadside parking area is located at the bottom of Churchill Drive, at the north end of Cedar Hill Road, near Shelbourne Street. You can drive another 1.5 km up the steep and winding Churchill Drive to the parking lot which overlooks the Blenkinsop Valley.

**Glendenning Road:** Very limited roadside parking is available at the end of Glendenning Road, which is accessed from Mount Douglas Cross Road.

**Hike Descriptions:**
**Irvine Trail** (moderate/1.6 km, one way): This signposted trail begins on Cordova Bay Road's west side, just south of the main parking lot, near Ash Road. At the Norn Trail junction consider a detour north to a fine viewpoint on Irvine Hill that overlooks Cordova Bay. The trail soon steepens and crosses Churchill Drive and continues to rise steadily. It leaves the lower elevation forest behind to enter a craggy Garry oak and arbutus hilltop. On the approach to the Mount Douglas summit the

trail becomes rough and traverses open rock, which can be slippery at times. Some short scrambling may be required. Finally the trail reaches the summit area, near the radio antenna. Allow 45 minutes to 1 hour to reach the summit.

There are three viewpoints at the top. One is on the east side, next to the radio antenna, another is at the end of Churchill Drive, at the parking area overlook. The main viewpoint is just to the west accessed along a paved, steep path. The Mount Douglas summit (227 m) features a 360-degree vista of the Saanich Peninsula, Victoria, Washington State's Cascade and Olympic mountains, the Malahat, the Sooke Hills and the Gulf Islands.

**Whittaker Trail** (moderate/3.8 km loop): One of the longest trails in the park, the Whittaker Trail winds completely around Mount Douglas, under a thick canopy of western red cedar, Douglas-fir, grand fir, Pacific dogwood and bigleaf maple. The route follows generally rolling terrain with some grades but nothing really strenuous. You can access the trail from the main parking lot by crossing Cordova Bay Road. The trail can be picked up at various other points along Cedar Hill Road and Cadboro Bay Road. Allow about 2 hours to complete the loop.

The Whittaker Trail connects with all of the major Mount Douglas trails. Figuring out exactly where you are, though, can be puzzling due to many unmarked and confusing trail intersections and side paths. You can stay on track by using the Mount Douglas summit as a reference point. For example, if you hike in a counter-clockwise direction, the summit will always be to your left.

An interesting section of the Whittaker Trail runs between the Mount Douglas summit and that of Little Mount Doug, on the park's northwest side. Side trails lead to the top of Little Mount Doug where there are excellent views and spring wildflowers. Old mine workings are located at the junction with the Harrop Trail and the Tod Trail (a strenuous route off the Mercer Trail). The Mercer Trail, a link to the Lochside Trail, comes in from Blenkinsop Road. Near this junction, look for a blowdown caused by a typhoon in the mid-1950s (started in Guam). From the Harrop Trail, just north of where the Whittaker and Glendenning trails meet, a short but arduous scramble over steep, exposed, rocky bluffs will bring you to the viewpoint at the summit parking area.

**Merriman Trail**: (moderate/1.3 km, one way): From the north end of the main parking lot take the Merriman Trail along the bluff, cross Cordova Bay Road and turn right, briefly sharing the route with the Whittaker Trail, to a quarry (on the left), where you cut left. The trail is obvious at the beginning, with easy hiking in the lower section. The route crosses the Norn

Trail and then narrows and starts to climb, passing close to Churchill Drive (near a connecting link to the Irvine Trail) and then turns west to the Whittaker Trail.

**Norn Trail** (easy/1.7 km, one way): This trail is well defined and provides easy hiking on fairly level ground with some slight grades. It roughly parallels Cordova Bay Road passing through tall timber. Access is just north of the bottom parking area on Churchill Drive, at several points along the Whittaker Trail or via the Irvine Trail.

**Beach Trail** (easy/860 m, one way): From the parking area at the base of Churchill Drive you can follow this delightful trail that parallels Douglas Creek, crosses Ash Road and ends at the sandy Cordova Bay beach, below the main parking lot. During periods of extremely low tides, it's possible to extend your hike another 10 km north to Island View Beach. (See page 155.) The Beach Trail accesses the Douglas Trail, which runs through the forest on the park's eastern boundary to Ash Road.

**Worth Noting:**

- The thick forests of Mount Douglas are home to a variety of birds. Watch for Anna's Hummingbirds, woodpeckers, and Varied Thrushes. Mount Douglas is one of Vancouver Island's major stopovers for migratory birds, with hundreds of species documented. These include warblers, Rufous-sided Towhees, Western Tanagers, White-crowned Sparrows and Lazuli Buntings.

- In the spring, the forests, meadows and rocky outcrops on Mount Douglas offer a brilliant display of native wildflowers. Look for Hooker's onion, spring gold, camas, satin flowers, shooting stars, western buttercup, white fawn lilies, chocolate lilies and others. Mount Douglas is one of only 21 sites in BC where the rare purple sanicle grows. This "red-listed" species suffers from competition from invasive plants (like Scotch broom) and habitat loss.

- Please stay on designated trails to protect sensitive vegetation. Do not pick any wildflowers.

- Use caution when crossing Cordova Bay Road.

- The Friends of Mount Douglas is a society formed to ensure the park's natural state and to preserve the original park boundaries as set out by Sir James Douglas in 1889.

- The signposted Mercer Trail links Mount Douglas with the Lochside Trail via Blenkinsop Road and Lohbrunner Road (east). (See page 153.)

**Nearby:**
**Two tiny Saanich parks** east of Mount Douglas Park are worth a visit. Both are excellent birdwatching destinations. Short trails lead to spectacular Haro Strait and San Juan Islands views. The parks have limited parking and toilets. No cyclists are permitted.

**Glencoe Cove-Kwatsech Park** (3.6 ha): Accessed off Ferndale Road, parking is limited on Gordon Point Drive. There are aboriginal burial cairns, shell middens, rare plants (including prickly pear and bearded owl-clover), Garry oaks, a cormorant rookery, two small, secluded beaches and a pocket cove. Ferndale Forest, on Vantreight Drive's east side, is also part of the park. The Friends of Glencoe Cove-Kwatsech Park was established in 1995 to protect, preserve and restore the native plants and archeological sites at Glencoe Cove.

**Arbutus Cove Park** (1.8 ha): Accessed off Gordon Head Road, parking is limited on Arbutus Cove Lane. There is a picnic site and benches along the bluff. A set of steps accesses the beach. The paved paths are wheelchair accessible.

Mount Douglas was first known as the "hill of cedars" to the local Songhees people. Later, after these same people harvested lengthy cedar planks from its forests to construct the palisades around Fort Victoria, its title was formalized as "Cedar Hill". Still later, when Captain G.H. Richards was standardizing local geographic nomenclature, he called any rise under one thousand feet a hill, and any above, a mountain. He made an exception for Mount Douglas, as he did not wish to "lower" the Governor. "Douglas Hill does not sound well" he explained.

Several of the Mount Douglas trails are named after local pioneer families. This parkland was originally set aside in 1858 by Governor Sir James Douglas as a Government Reserve and has been protected as a Crown Trust since 1889. We can credit early Victoria mayor, Bert Todd, with the foresight to construct an "auto road" to the summit as a tourist attraction. In late 1992 the park was transferred to Saanich.

Photo: Di Chawner

*Stop and look up*

# 13. University of Victoria

Photo: Aldyth Hunter

Finnerty Gardens (2.6 ha) has numerous trails through the garden which features over 200 types of rhododendrons and azaleas as well as over 1600 varieties of shrubs and trees. There are resting benches and three quiet ponds. April and May are the best times to view the rhododendrons, many of which were started from seed. Some specimens are over 70 years old. The gardens are open daily during daylight hours and there is no admission charge. Allow at least an hour to tour the gardens. Parking Lot 6, near the chapel and closest to the gardens, is wheelchair accessible.

## 13. University of Victoria

**Highlights:** The many wooded areas and open fields and grasslands at the University of Victoria are the setting for a 4.5 km loop hike that winds around the campus perimeter. From the Alumni Trail, you may visit the magnificent rhododendrons and plant displays at Finnerty Gardens or explore Mystic Vale, an ecological protection area on the university's east side. Extend your walk with a climb up Mount Tolmie, one of Victoria's best viewpoints. There are great opportunities for nature appreciation and birdwatching.

**Difficulty/Distance:** easy to moderate/0.5 km to 4.5 km loop, plus

**Access to the Alumni Trail:** Our starting point for the Alumni Trail is near Parking Lot 10, reached via West Campus Gate off Gordon Head Road or the Ring Road (University Drive). Parking is free after 6 pm weekdays and on weekends and holidays. The trail may also be accessed at numerous places along its route. Most of the level sections of the Alumni Trail are wheelchair accessible, though on some grades one may require assistance.

**Hike Description:**

**Alumni Trail** (easy to moderate/4.5 km loop): Near Parking Lot 10 find the trail where it crosses the parking lot entrance road and head south. At the Garry oak meadow, near the university's southwest corner, is the cutoff trail to Mount Tolmie. (For a description of Mount Tolmie, see page 71.)

Keep left at the Mount Tolmie junction and follow the Alumni Trail through the fields. The route parallels Cedar Hill Cross Road to the sign-posted trail (on the left) to Finnerty Gardens. Stop at the gardens sign and turn left to continue your walk through the beauty and tranquility of the garden, past the pond and the University Interfaith Chapel and exit at University Drive. In the Spring the rhododendron and other horticultural displays here are dazzling.

From the Finnerty Gardens exit, head east at the Alumni Trail sign, and cross University Drive to the dense forest of South Woods. Next are two junctions fairly close together. Keep left at both by following the signs. One of the right trails leads across Cedar Hill Cross Road to Oak Bay's Henderson Park (8.5 ha) and a 1 km forested trail around the golf course.

The Alumni Trail swings towards Ring Road and then turns right along the southwest fringe of large Parking Lot 1. At the Mystic Vale signpost there is a choice of routes. The left path is the Mystic Vale bypass, which skirts Parking Lot 1 through the adjacent forest and runs past campus housing to Sinclair Road. Keep right at the junction to reach Mystic Vale (4.6 ha), accessed via a long, steep set of wooden steps. This ecological protection area within the University of Victoria property features a lush wooded ravine harbouring one of Victoria's last remaining moist Douglas-fir forests. The firs share the ravine with bigleaf maples, dogwood, yew trees and a plethora of shrubs and mosses. Be alert. Wandering cougars have been spotted in and around Mystic Vale.

At the bottom of the steps swing left along Hobbs Creek to the ravine's north end, near Hobbs Street. Climb the bank and walk a short distance along the road to locate the trail up a steep hill. At the top, walk along the pavement to a trail on the right, follow it and then cut through a small parking area and past university residences to Sinclair Road. Turn left and take the sidewalk up the hill.

At Finnerty Road swing left and walk behind the bookstore and McKinnon Gym on a paved sidewalk and cross Gabriola Road. Beyond a sports field the path curves north to parallel McKenzie Avenue and passes Centennial Stadium. Turn south and cross McGill Road to a grassy field. The trail enters a wooded area near Bowker Creek, an important habitat for songbirds, woodpeckers and owls, and winds up a slight grade to Parking Lot 10.

**Worth Noting:**

- The Alumni Trail, a popular jogging route, is partly chip, gravel and pavement.

- Campus woodlands include Douglas-fir, Garry oak, arbutus and bigleaf maple trees.

- Look for spring wildflowers like trillium, camas, shooting stars and vanilla leaf in the grassy fields and along the boulevards.

- Hutton's Vireos reside on the fringe of Mystic Vale. Listen and search for these elusive birds in the spring through early summer and again in the late summer through early fall. The ravine is home to Barred Owls, Great-horned Owls, ravens, Bald Eagles, Cooper's Hawks and a variety of woodpeckers.

**Access to Mount Tolmie:**

**By Foot**: As for the Alumni Trail to the Mount Tolmie Trail cutoff, on UVIC's southwest corner. Walk to pedestrian light at the corner of Cedar Hill Cross Road and Gordon Head Road and cross Cedar Hill Road. The Mount Tolmie trailhead is on the south side.

**By Road:** In Victoria, travel north on Shelbourne Street and turn right at the Cedar Hill Cross Road lights. Continue past Richmond Road to Mayfair Drive. Turn right. Park at any of the small, roadside parking spots along Mayfair Drive or the larger area at the summit. Only the level sections of the trails are wheelchair accessible. Mount Tolmie trails are open sunrise to sunset.

## Hike Description:

**Mount Tolmie Trails** (moderate/0.5 km to 2 km loop): Saanich's Mount Tolmie Park (18.3 ha) has several groomed trails that wind through a Garry oak and arbutus hilltop. You can create your own loop hike through wildflower meadows to the 120-m summit. Begin at the bottom, on Cedar Hill Cross Road, or higher up along Mayfair Drive. Trails on Mount Tolmie's east slope are slightly less steep than those on the west side. The magnificent view at the top offers a 360-degree panorama that includes Victoria, the Juan de Fuca Strait, the Olympic Mountains, the Sooke Hills, Mount Douglas, the Saanich Peninsula and the San Juan Islands. On a clear day you can see Mount Baker. The sunset here is unsurpassed.

## Worth Noting:

- Bicycles are not allowed on the Mount Tolmie trails.
- The park has picnic tables but no other facilities.
- Enjoy the seasonal meadow wildflowers but stay on the trails to protect fragile vegetation.
- Spring flowers include camas, fawn lilies and satin flowers (sometimes called grass widows).
- Watch for woodpeckers, Bewick's Wrens, Anna's Hummingbirds, Olive-sided Flycatchers, raptors and a variety of other birds. Early spring mornings are the best times for spotting migrant species. Golden-crowned Sparrows winter in the area.
- The park's drier terrain is habitat for alligator lizards. These creatures blend in perfectly with their surroundings, even when they are basking in summer sunlight on a rock outcrop.
- Mount Tolmie's open rock faces display evidence of striation (grooving) caused by glacier scouring thousands of years ago.
- The summit viewpoint and nearby lookout at the water reservoir are favourite places to enjoy the view.
- Mount Tolmie was named in 1934 after biologist Dr. William Fraser Tolmie, physician, botanist, linguist, ethnologist and legislator.

## Nearby:

The many trails in Mount Douglas Park are close to the University of Victoria. (See page 63 for a description.)

# 14. Cedar Hill Golf Course

Photo: Joyce Folbigg

Originally a dairy farm, Cedar Hill Golf Course was built in the 1920s as a 9-hole private course, which expanded in the 1950s to 18 holes. It was bought by Saanich in 1967 and reopened a few years later as Vancouver Island's very first municipal golf course.

## 14. Cedar Hill Golf Course

**Highlights:** In the heart of Saanich there is a delightful loop trail around the Cedar Hill Golf Course. The trail passes two small lakes popular with birdwatchers and the higher points of land along the way provide captivating views of Victoria and Juan de Fuca Strait. Hikers and joggers use this path.

**Difficulty/Distance:** moderate/3.6 km loop

**Access:** Parking is available at the Cedar Hill Community Recreation Centre, near the intersection of Cedar Hill Road and Finlayson Street, or go north at the intersection on Cedar Hill Road, turn left onto Doncaster Drive and left again on Derby Road to the Cedar Hill Golf Course clubhouse parking lot. The trail is open sunrise to sunset.

**Hike Description:**

A 3.6-km trail circles the Cedar Hill Golf Course and winds through gently rolling hills, open terrain and wooded areas with scattered patches of Douglas-fir trees and gnarled Garry oaks. The northern loop leads to King's Pond, with its abundant wildlife. Along the southern loop you will encounter some hills, including a sharp grade near beautiful Barwick Lake. The highest points along the trail offer great views of Victoria, the Juan de Fuca Strait and, on clear days, the stunning backdrop of the Olympic Mountains.

This combination hiking and jogging path is made up of chip bark, gravel and a paved section. You can hike only half of the route by cutting across the golf course on the marked trail that passes the clubhouse.

**Worth Noting:**

- King's Pond and Barwick Lake have viewing areas.
- Watch for Virginia Rails, Red-winged Blackbirds, mallards, American Widgeons and other ducks.
- There are numerous benches along the trail to watch the golfing action or just enjoy the scenery.
- The loop trail can be reached from many access points around the perimeter of the golf course.

**Nearby:**

**Mount Tolmie** and trails to its spectacular summit viewpoint are just a few blocks east of Cedar Hill Golf Course. (See page 71.)

**Playfair Park** can be accessed from the trail at Judge Place and Blenkinsop Road.

# 15. Victoria Waterfront

Photo: Aldyth Hunter

# 15. Victoria Waterfront

**Highlights:** This world class stroll, along the Juan de Fuca Strait, begins at the 0.8-km-long Ogden Point breakwater and features one of Victoria's most beautiful seascape walks.

**Difficulty/Distance:** easy/3 km, one way

**Cautions:** Dogs are permitted off-leash from Douglas Street to Clover Point.

**Access:** Near Dallas Road and Dock Street in James Bay there is a pay parking lot near the Ogden Point breakwater. Free parking is available along Dallas Road and at Clover Point. Public toilets are available at the end of Cook Street.

**Ogden Point to Oak Bay**

**Hike Descriptions:**
Begin the walk at the Ogden Point breakwater, in James Bay. The 0.8-km-long breakwater dates back to 1913 and was constructed from rock quarried at Albert Head. The breakwater is a popular birdwatching spot and a great destination for just getting wind-blown. Off-shore is Brotchie Ledge beacon, scene of many marine disasters. The light is a prominent geographical reference point for pilots, scuba divers, fisher-men, and government agencies.

From the breakwater head east along the seawall, past Holland Point Park (5 ha) and the Harrison model yacht pond, named after the mayor of Victoria in the 1950s. The cliffside walk, with numerous beach access points, parallels Dallas Road and offers magnificent views of the Olympic Mountains and the Juan de Fuca Strait. Near Paddon Street there is a bench in a sheltered nook. Offshore is Glimpse Reef. Nearby Fonyo Beach is named after Steve Fonyo, whose Journey for Lives run ended there in 1985.

At the foot of Douglas Street you have three choices. You could cross the road to visit the "Mile 0" monument, marking the western terminus of the Trans Canada Highway and the Vancouver Island section of the Trans-Canada Trail. A bronze statue of Terry Fox was erected nearby in 2005 to commemorate his courageous Marathon of Hope run. From here detour up Douglas Street for a soft ice cream cone at the Beacon Drive-In Restaurant, and then cross Douglas Street to enter Beacon Hill Park. Your second option is to take the stairs near the foot of Douglas Street and hike along the beach, or, thirdly, continue east on the cliffside walk.

The bluffs, particularly near Horseshoe Bay, display evidence of the inces-sant erosion on the cliff face, and of the sometimes controversial attempts to stop that erosion by artificial berms, drains, and the planting of native shrubs. The latter include Nootka rose, snowberry, red currant, ocean spray, mock orange, Saskatoon berry and Garry oak.

Halfway to Clover Point you will reach a shelter, near Finlayson Point. There is a monument honouring Marilyn Bell, who swam the Juan de Fuca Strait in 1956. At the end of Cook Street there are public washrooms. In the spring, you will see the yellow gorse in bloom. It is an introduced species like the Scotch broom that it resembles.

As you approach Clover Point you are likely to see colourful kites over-head. Those really big kites, with humans attached, are paragliders, akin to hang-gliders. Take special note of the birds in the air and on the waves. Clover Point is one of the best places around Victoria to spot migrating spe-cies. Glaucous-winged Gulls, Harlequin Ducks and pigeons are common.

**Worth Noting:**

- A special pet fountain is located just east of Douglas Street.
- The Capital Bike and Walk Society publishes *Walk Downtown Victoria*, a pamphlet describing many of Victoria's urban walks. These range from 15 minutes to an hour. Contact: capitalbikeandwalk.org for more details.

**Nearby:**

**Ross Bay Cemetery** (11 ha) is adorned with many exotic trees and has been the final resting-place of many of Victoria's prominent citizens since 1873. It is a fine example of a typical Victorian cemetery, with formal land-scaping and a variety of interesting tombstones. To reach this historic graveyard continue east from Clover Point along a seaside promenade, which can be spectacular and sometimes closed during rough weather. NO dogs are allowed in the cemetery.

**The Chinese Cemetery** (1.4 ha), off King George Terrace at the foot of Crescent Street, is Canada's oldest Chinese cemetery. The land was origi-nally purchased in 1903 by the Chinese Consolidated Benevolent Associa-tion. In 1996, the cemetery was designated a National Historic Site. At Harling Point there are spring wildflowers and great views across Juan de Fuca Strait to the Olympic Mountains.

Continuing along the waterfront to Beach Drive you enter the municipality of Oak Bay. Available from the Oak Bay Parks and Recreation is a pam-phlet on "Scenic Walks" in the municipality (recreation.oakbaybc.org). Do not miss Gonzales Hill, Walbran and Anderson Hill Parks, Willows Beach and Cattle Point. This will end your eastward walk close to the Uni-versity of Victoria. ( See page 68.)

## Ogden Point to West Bay

From Ogden Point breakwater, turn left and walk along Dallas Road to Montreal Street, where there is a blue and orange Walk Victoria sign. Follow the signs to Fisherman's Wharf which is worth pausing to explore. Have fish and chips or an ice cream cone at the popular Barb's Place. Look across the harbour which is where your walk will take you. Victoria Harbour is a busy working harbour. Float planes, dancing ferries, dragon boat racing, whale- watching zodiacs, classic boat festivals and Swiftsure yacht racing all vie for the space and attention. Return to the street, turn left and continue to follow the signs, all around the Inner Harbour, past the Parliament buildings, the Fairmont Empress Hotel, the old Custom House to the blue Johnson Street Bridge. Cross the bridge to the Songhees lands, where the trail becomes Westsong Way and continue to West Bay Marina. If you become tired at any point along the way, take the little ferry (there are eleven of them) across the harbour to pick up the walkway again.

## Nearby:
At West Bay you are in Esquimalt which has some real gems to explore. Look for Fleming Beach, Kinsmen Gorge and Highrock Park with the Royal Canadian Navy cairn, and Saxe Point, a beautiful bayside park with forest paths and ocean views.

Sir James Douglas named Clover Point as he landed here from the *Beaver* in 1843. Presumably he saw reddish-purple flowers of springbank clover, a perennial native species and food source for local indigenous people. Other clovers are introduced species.

~ ~ ~

Beacon Hill Park (75 ha) features lawns, fields, flower garden and native and imported trees. A variety of paths intersect the park. Burial mounds, constructed of large granite rocks, may be seen on Beacon Hill's southern slope, below the flagpole. This area is carpeted with blue camas in May.

~ ~ ~

Dallas Road was named for Alexander Grant Dallas, chief factor with the Hudson's Bay Company. Finlayson Point was named for Roderick Finlayson, Hudson's Bay Chief Factor at Victoria, 1844-1872. Here a plaque advises that this was once the site of an ancient fortified village. The plaque also marks the site of a gun battery during the Russo-Turkish war (1878-1892).

# Swan Lake and Christmas Hill

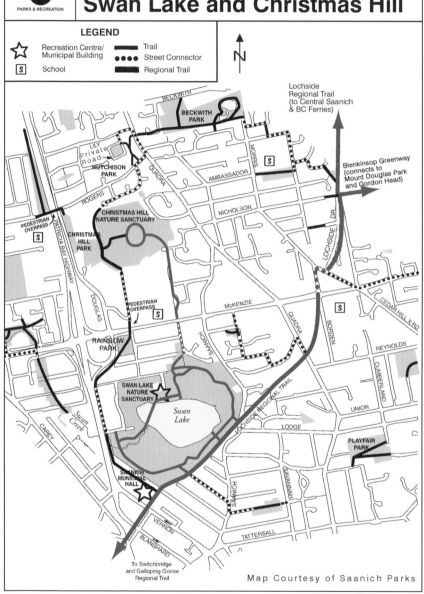

Map Courtesy of Saanich Parks

## 16. Swan Lake and Christmas Hill

**Highlights:** The Swan Lake/Christmas Hill Nature Sanctuary is located in Saanich and features two diverse hikes. The Swan Lake Loop winds around picturesque Swan Lake (10 ha) on a partly chip bark, gravel and boardwalk trail. The marshland, fields and thickets surrounding the lake are perfect for bird watching. The trail to Christmas Hill climbs to a protected Garry oak forest with seasonal wildflowers and several viewpoints. The Swan Lake Nature House and information centre offers interpretive programs. Visit the nearby native garden. You can even purchase grain for feeding the ducks.

**Difficulty/Distance:** easy to moderate/1.3 km, one way to 2.5 km loop

**Cautions:** Christmas Hill Trails are steep and rocky.

**Access:** For Swan Lake, from Victoria take Blanshard Street then Highway #17 (Pat Bay) north to McKenzie Avenue. Turn right (east) to Rainbow Street. Swing right and continue to the intersection with Ralph Street. Turn left (east) at the sanctuary signpost. The parking area is near the end of Ralph Street. If traveling west along McKenzie Avenue be aware there is no left turn at Rainbow Street. Instead, turn left at Nelthorpe Street and then right via Sevenoaks Road to Rainbow Street. Sections of the Swan Lake Loop are wheelchair-accessible.

For Christmas Hill, travel as for the Swan Lake to the end of Ralph Street. The signposted trail starts at the northeast end of the parking lot. Both trails are open from sunrise to sunset.

**Hike Descriptions:**

**Swan Lake Loop** (easy/2.5 km loop): The trail begins at the Nature House as a wood chip path and encircles the lake. The path crosses Swan and Blenkinsop creeks en route. A floating bridge with benches is one highlight.

The trail accesses a bird blind and two wharves that allow visitors to more easily view the natural surroundings. Take your time and be observant. Many bird and duck species are found here, some resident, others migratory. The thick growth of cattails and duckweed around the lake is a perfect refuge. Painted turtles, river otters and muskrat are occasionally seen in and around Swan Lake. There is an impressive stand of giant cottonwoods on the south shore.

**Christmas Hill** (moderate/1.3 km, one way): The hike to Christmas Hill from the Swan Lake Nature House leads to a fragile Garry oak forest and rocky outcrops. The surrounding areas are covered with lichens, mosses,

79

ferns and seasonal wildflowers. Watch for a variety of butterflies from late spring through the summer.

From the Nature Centre parking lot, hike east, then north to a marked junction. Turn left and follow the Christmas Hill signposts. Take Nelthorpe Street to McKenzie Avenue and the pedestrian light. On McKenzie Avenue's north side the path again briefly joins Nelthorpe Street. Continue north to cross Nicholson Street. Note the small stand of old-growth Douglas-fir. From this point on, the way is narrow, rocky and steep to the top, where the trail circles the summit to three viewpoints. There is one of Swan Lake, another of Central Saanich and the spectacular 360-degree vista from the Christmas Hill summit (122 m) that takes in all of Victoria and environs.

**Worth Noting:**

- Stay on the trails to minimize damage to the area's fragile ecosystems.
- NO dogs and no bicycles are permitted on the trails.
- A wide variety of interpretive programs is offered at the Swan Lake Nature House, including bird watches, junior naturalists programs and topics about everything from archaeology to reptiles. Contact: swanlake.bc.ca for information.
- Along Swan Lake's south side you can connect with the Lochside Regional Trail and then the Galloping Goose Trail. (See pages 152 and 146.)

**Nearby:**
**Playfair Park** (3.7 ha) is "a jewel" within the Saanich Parks system. Over 250 species of plants grow here, including a seasonal display of magnificent rhododendrons. The parking lot is at the end of Rock Street, accessed off Quadra Street. The park has several trails, a picnic area and toilets.

**Beckwith Park** (9 ha) This park features a winding wood chip trail along its perimeter, Garry oak trees and two lovely ponds. There are opportunities to observe birds and other wildlife. The large parking lot on Beckwith Avenue is accessed off Quadra Street. There are wheelchair accessible toilets and a picnic area.

Swan Lake is fed by Blenkinsop Lake, via Blenkinsop Creek. The lake is drained by Swan Creek, which flows under Douglas Street and McKenzie Avenue to join Colquitz Creek near Hyacinth Park. Swan Creek and Lake are named after James Gilchrist Swan, a well-known early ethnologist.

**Binoculars**

A pair of light 6, 7 or 8 power binoculars, that provide a bright and sharp image as soon as you lift them to your eyes, can really enhance your hiking experience and your appreciation of the feathered world around you. Avoid heavy binoculars with larger magnification and those with a zoom feature as you will find yourself struggling to obtain a sharp image and hold the target in your field of view. Birds seldom stay still for very long and heavier, more powerful binoculars, and those that are difficult to bring into focus will frustrate you.

# 17. Colquitz River

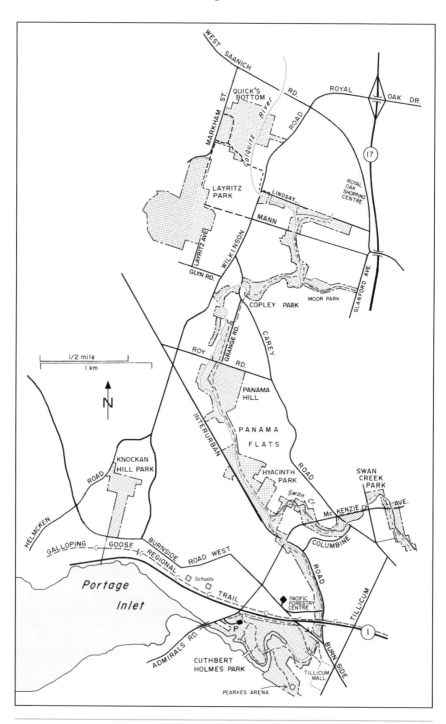

## 17. Colquitz River

**Highlights:** Saanich's Colquitz River Linear Park and adjoining Cuthbert Holmes Park connect urban and rural parks that stretch from the Portage Inlet north to the Elk Lake area. Hikers can explore the scenic trail that parallels the Colquitz River through working farmland, commercial areas, residential housing and greenbelts. This is a fragile environment that includes open forests, delicate wetlands, Garry oak hilltops, sensitive eco-systems and streams with spawning populations of trout and salmon. The trails within Cuthbert Holmes Park (19.9 ha) wind through an urban mixed forest to a river estuary, grassy fields and open meadows along the Colquitz River. Birdwatching and nature viewing opportunities are endless.

**Difficulty/Distance:** easy/2 km loop to 5 km, one way

**Cautions:** Use caution at all street crossings.

**Access:** To Colquitz River Linear Park: From Victoria, take Highway #1 (Trans-Canada) to Tillicum Road intersection and swing left. At the Burnside Road West traffic lights, turn right and then make an immediate left into the Tillicum Mall. Park in the lot's northwest corner (on the right) close to the Cuthbert Holmes Park trailhead. The Colquitz River Linear Park can be accessed at a number of points along its length. Parking is extremely limited at the Colquitz River Trail's north end. Most of the trail from Tillicum Mall north to Hyacinth Park is wheelchair accessible. From downtown Victoria, allow 15 minutes driving time.

**Access:** To Cuthbert Holmes Park: From Victoria, take Highway #1 (Trans-Canada) west to the Admirals Road lights. Turn left (south) onto Admirals Road. The parking lot is on the left, as soon as you turn off the highway. Another entry to the park is off Dysart Road at Ker Avenue, from behind the G.R. Pearkes Community Recreation Centre (off Arena Road) or at the trailhead at the Tillicum Mall parking lot. The paved main trail is wheelchair accessible. From downtown Victoria, allow 15 minutes driving time.

**Hike Descriptions:**

**Colquitz River Linear Park** (easy/approximately 5 km, one way): From the Tillicum Mall parking lot, take the Cuthbert Holmes Park access trail north to a fork. Ignore the path to the left that crosses the Colquitz River on a sturdy bridge; instead, keep north, under the Highway #1 overpass and the Galloping Goose Trail bridge, to cross Burnside Road West. A side path, on the left, climbs to the Pacific Forestry Centre. The gravel trail winds alongside the Colquitz River and in this stretch, small bridges and stepping stones assist with some creek crossings. You will pass under McKenzie Avenue and cross Interurban Road.

At the confluence of the Colquitz River and Swan Creek, near Violet Avenue, the Swan Creek Trail cuts off, to the right. (See Nearby.) Cross Marigold Road to enter Hyacinth Park (5 ha). The trail skirts the Panama Flats wetland, which always seems to attract birds, and climbs a bit to pass Panama Hill and Pond, both within Panama Hill Park (9 ha).

North of Roy Road, turn right and follow a short stretch of Gerda Road to Grange Road, then turn left and continue north to Carey Road. Across the street, look for the hard-to-see entrance to Copley Park (5.4 ha). This park is divided into east and west sections, each on opposite sides of Carey Road.

At Moor Park (1 ha), just over a metal bridge that spans the Colquitz River, turn east and continue through Industrial Buffer Park (3.4 ha) to Glanford Avenue. The Colquitz River Trail heads north over Mann Avenue and soon forks. Turn right for Glanford Avenue, just south of the Royal Oak Shopping Centre. Keep straight ahead for Lindsay Street and then swing left on Lindsay to Wilkinson Road. Two trailheads for Quick's Bottom are just north of here, along Wilkinson Road. (See Nearby.)

**Cuthbert Holmes Park** (easy/2 km loop): From the Admirals Road parking area follow the paved main trail to a fork. The main trail runs through the centre of the park to a Colquitz River bridge. Turn right onto the narrower bark-mulch trail, which enters the woods dominated by Douglas-fir and grand fir and eventually meets and runs alongside the Colquitz River. A side path, on the right, angles off to the river estuary and tidal marsh. Walk quietly and you might see a Great Blue Heron stalking the tidal shallows.

Continue east along the riverbank, avoiding any paths on the left as there are many unmarked side paths, and soon you will reach Heron Bridge and foot access to Dysart Road. The river trail passes a disused heron rookery and curves north to rejoin the main trail near the previously mentioned Colquitz River bridge. Turn right onto the main trail and cross the bridge. Near the Pearkes Arena access trail, which comes in on the right, the path enters an open, bushy area and then swings north, close to Tillicum Mall. Just past the mall parking lot trail access and a little before the highway overpass, turn left to cross the concrete bridge over the Colquitz River. The Colquitz River Linear Trail begins nearby. To return to the Admirals Road parking area, hike west parallel to Highway #1 with a large meadow on the left.

**Worth Noting:**

- Do not remove any native vegetation and avoid trampling streamside areas. Panama Pond and Panama Hill are sensitive regions.

- At Cuthbert Holmes Park look for native grasses and a variety of shrubs such as wild rose, hawthorn and blackberry. Spring wildflowers include white fawn lilies, lady slippers, Easter lilies, western trillium and camas. At the Colquitz River estuary you might see Hooded Mergansers, mallards, teal, Great Blue Herons or Green Herons.

**Nearby:**

**Swan Creek Park** (10.3 ha): From along the Colquitz River Trail at Hyacinth Park (near the confluence of the Colquitz River and Swan Creek) you can access the Swan Creek Trail. Turn east to follow tiny Swan Creek all the way to the Ralph Street allotment gardens. This involves a short section along the heavily-travelled McKenzie Avenue.

**Knockan Hill Park** (9.3 ha): Accessed along Burnside Road West, the trailhead is next to a 1930s stucco house called Stranton Lodge, a designated heritage house. Park on High Street, near the Strawberry Vale Community Hall. The 0.5-km (one way) trail climbs the driveway, past Stranton Lodge (Hall Cottage) to hilltop meadows and an open rocky summit with good views to the north and east. Spring wildflowers are abundant. There are a few benches. The Friends of Knockan Hill Park was established to preserve the park's natural character and its flora and fauna.

**Quick's Bottom** (15 ha): NO dogs allowed here. This is a wildlife sanctuary, intersected by the Colquitz River, is one of the few remaining marshlands close to Victoria. Quick's Bottom is accessed off Markham Street or Wilkinson Road. Limited roadside parking is found on Greenlea Drive, off Wilkinson Road. A 1.5-km (35-minute) trail loops through the marsh and provides a close look at area birds, wildlife and wetland vegetation. The Victoria Natural History Society constructed the birdwatching blind at the marsh's southwest end, near the Saanich municipal nursery. There are benches en route. Take your time. More than one birder has added to a life list here. This bottomland is a depression remaining from the glacial age.

**Layritz Park** (29 ha): The park is accessed off Wilkinson Road, then via Glyn Road and Layritz Avenue, via the pedestrian right-of-way off Wilkinson Road and Mann Avenue, or off Markham Street. Trails wind through Garry oak meadows on the park's wooded west side. Layritz Park and nearby Quick's Bottom are great spots to observe early spring migratory birds.

# 18. Thetis Lake

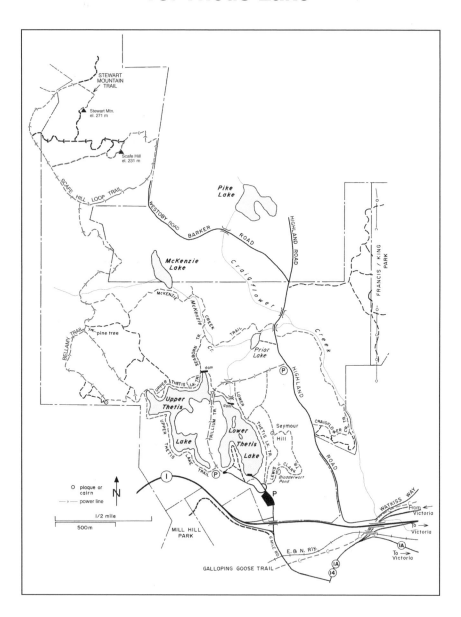

## 18. Thetis Lake

**Highlights:** The trails at Thetis Lake Regional Park (831 ha) can be hiked any time of the year. Located in View Royal/Langford, this CRD park has 47 km of trails with varying degrees of difficulty. Many paths interconnect so it is easy to plot your own circular hike. The park offers brilliant displays of spring wildflowers, outcrops of moss-covered bedrock and mixed forests of Douglas-fir, arbutus and Garry oak. There are excellent opportunities for nature appreciation and wildlife viewing, all within a natural lake and swamp ecosystem.

**Difficulty/Distance:** easy to strenuous/1.3 km to 7 km and up, one way

**Cautions:** Seymour Hill, north side has very steep sections. Parts of the trail are narrow and rocky.

**Access:** From Victoria, take Highway #1 (Trans-Canada) west and turn off at Exit 10 (Colwood) and follow the Old Island Highway to the Six Mile Road traffic lights. Turn right and continue straight ahead to the main parking lot. Additional parking is available at the smaller West Beach lot. Parking is free from October to April. Fees apply May to September. Contact CRD Parks for current information on fees and season passes. Limited roadside parking is available off Highland Road near Prior Lake, at the eastern trailhead for the Trillium Trail. From Victoria, allow 20 minutes driving time. The park is open from sunrise to sunset.

**Hike Descriptions:**

**Lewis J. Clark Trail** (moderate/1.4 km, one way): This trail to one of the park's best viewpoints starts at the main parking lot kiosk. Take the trail on the right and follow the signposts. The route climbs, first through a Douglas-fir forest, then up through drier woodlands of Garry oak and arbutus. Expect some up and down hiking en route. At the junction with the Seymour Hill Trail, swing right (north) and hike the final pitch to the top.

At the Seymour Hill summit (141 m) the view over Thetis Lake is spectacular. A directional cairn constructed by the Thetis Lake Nature Sanctuary Association in 1968 pinpoints local hills and mountains, including Mount Work and Mount Finlayson. Spring wildflowers abound on this hilltop.

To return to the starting point, retrace your steps or take the southern section of the Seymour Hill Trail. A third option is to tackle the rugged trail down Seymour Hill's north side. Hike with caution if you choose the latter. Keep left on your descent until, at the bottom, you reach the trail along Lower Thetis Lake's east side that leads south and back to the parking lot. Allow approximately 1 to 1.5 hours for a return hike.

**Seymour Hill Trail** (moderate/1.3 km, one way): This is another way to the top of Seymour Hill. Take the middle trail from the main parking lot and climb to the summit viewpoint, just beyond the junction with the Lewis J. Clark Trail. See the Lewis J. Clark Trail description for additional details.

The Seymour Hill Trail continues north, down several steep inclines. Keep left at any junctions and you will eventually reach the lakeside trail that parallels Lower Thetis Lake's east shore. Swing left (south) for the parking lot. A return hike takes about 1 to 1.5 hours.

**Two Lake Loop** (moderate/4.5 km loop): The most popular hike at the park snakes around both Upper and Lower Thetis Lake. From the main parking lot, head north on the trail that parallels Lower Thetis Lake's east side. Halfway to Upper Thetis Lake's west end you can cut your hike short by turning left (south) onto the Trillium Trail, crossing the culvert bridge between the lakes and returning to the start.

**Trillium Trail** (easy/2 km, one way) follows a fire access road from Highland Road, just south of Prior Lake, to the West Beach parking lot. It is a multi-use hiking, cycling and equestrian trail.

To continue the Two Lake Loop take the trail around Upper Thetis Lake to the west end and weave back along the lake's southern shore. Take the time to investigate some of the numerous side paths that sneak down to the lakeside. Watch for waterfowl. The lakes are haunts for mallards, Canada Geese, Great Blue Herons and other resident and migratory species. Allow about 1.5 to 2 hours to complete the loop around the lakes.

**Thetis Lake to Scafe Hill** (moderate to strenuous/7 km, one way): Trails access the park's more remote spots, but if you venture into these regions, know your directions. This isolated part of the park, northwest of the lakes, has numerous confusing old roads, side paths and unmarked trails and junctions. Some lead to private property. Please keep to the designated trails.

From the main parking lot, follow the lake loop trail along Lower Thetis Lake's east side, cross the Trillium Trail to the Seaborn Trail junction and turn right (north) to the McKenzie Creek Trail junction.

**McKenzie Creek Trail** (moderate/2.9 km, one way) is an east/west hiking corridor stretching from Highland Road, north of Prior Lake, to the Bellamy Trail, the fire access road/trail to Scafe Hill and Stewart Mountain. The trail twists and turns along McKenzie Lake's outlet stream. Spring brings forth a profusion of swamp lantern (skunk cabbage) in low-lying wetter areas. In the shady forest look for western red cedar and hemlock and savour the verdant hues of the lichens and mosses. Near McKenzie Lake there are numerous gullies to negotiate.

For Scafe Hill turn left from the Seaborn Trail onto the McKenzie Creek Trail and head west to the fire access road (Bellamy Trail) that roughly parallels the park's western boundary. Turn right and hike north for Scafe Hill (231 m) and Stewart Mountain (271 m).

**Craigflower Creek Trail** (moderate/2 km, one way): From the limited parking area on Highland Road walk north to the Craigflower Creek trailhead, on the right a little before the next bridge. A scenic trail winds through forests and wetlands along Craigflower Creek and loops south back to Highland Road. Parts of the route may be muddy in wet weather. The stream was once called Deadman Creek.

**Worth Noting:**

- Spring wildflowers on rocky hilltops include satin flowers, camas, shooting stars, lilies, stonecrop and field chickweed.
- Do not pick wildflowers and stay on the marked trails.
- The park has swimming beaches, picnic areas and toilets. The main beaches are very busy in the summer.
- Bicycles and horses are permitted only on designated routes. These include the Trillium Trail, the fire access road/trail extending north to south along the Thetis Lake Park's western boundary and the trail off Highland Road that links to Francis/King Park.

**Nearby:**
A short 1 km hiking trail runs south from Thetis Lake to link with Mill Hill. (See page 90.) The Galloping Goose Trail can be accessed from Six Mile Road or Watkiss Way.

The Thetis Park Nature Sanctuary Association was formed in 1957 to protect Thetis Lake and environs from encroaching postwar development. Founding member and naturalist Dr. Lewis J. Clark wrote a series of field guides to wildflowers of the Pacific Northwest. The Lewis J. Clark Trail bears his name. The Jessie Woollett Memorial, near the park entrance, commemorates Jessie Woollett, also a TPNSA founding member. Ron Seaborn, for whom another connecting trail is named, is credited with the early mapping of the park's trails. Thetis Lake Park became Canada's first nature sanctuary in 1958. It was transferred from the City of Victoria to CRD Parks in 1993.

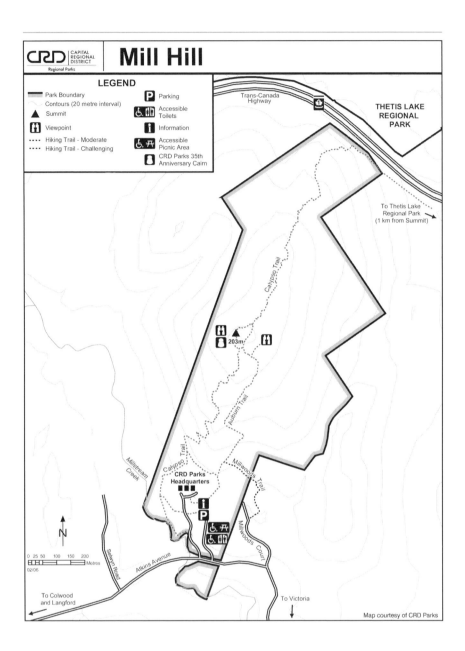

# Mill Hill

CRD | CAPITAL REGIONAL DISTRICT
Regional Parks

## LEGEND

- Park Boundary
- Contours (20 metre interval)
- ▲ Summit
- Viewpoint
- •••• Hiking Trail - Moderate
- •••• Hiking Trail - Challenging

- P Parking
- Accessible Toilets
- i Information
- Accessible Picnic Area
- CRD Parks 35th Anniversary Cairn

Trans-Canada Highway

THETIS LAKE REGIONAL PARK

To Thetis Lake Regional Park (1 km from Summit)

Calypso Trail

203m

Auburn Trail

Millstream Creek

Calypso Trail

CRD Parks Headquarters

Millwoods Trail

Millwoods Court

N

0 25 50 100 150 200 Metres
02/06

Selwyn Road

Atkins Avenue

To Colwood and Langford

To Victoria

Map courtesy of CRD Parks

# 19. Mill Hill

**Highlights**: The CRD's Mill Hill Regional Park (61 ha) is nc sonal wildflowers. There are over 100 varieties here, including ⅃ . cies, the most of any CRD park. Challenging trails climb to the top of Mɪ⊔ Hill where you will discover an excellent panorama of Esquimalt Harbour, Victoria and environs. Part of one trail meanders along the wetlands near Millstream Creek.

**Difficulty/Distance:** moderate/about 1 km, one way

**Cautions:** The summit trails are steep in places and made up of loose gravel and rock, which may be slippery and difficult for young children. There are open rock sections that can be slick in wet weather. Watch for protruding roots.

**Access:** From Victoria follow Highway #1 (Trans-Canada) and take Exit 14 to Langford and drive south on Veterans Memorial Parkway. Turn left onto Hoffman Avenue to a four-way-stop. Turn right on Winster Road then left onto Atkins Avenue. Continue approximately 1 km to cross the Millstream Creek bridge and past the entrance to CRD Park Headquarters, watch for the signposted park entrance on the left. From Victoria, allow 25 minutes driving time. The gate is open 8 am - 8 pm, April to October; 8 am - 5 pm, October to April. Park trails are not wheelchair accessible but the picnic area and toilets near the parking lot are.

**Hike Descriptions:**

**Auburn Trail** (moderate/760 m, one way): This trail, shorter and less of a grade than the Calypso Trail, begins at the parking lot's north end. Keep right at the fork a short distance in. A left down this side path connects with the Calypso Trail. Beyond this point, the trail rises steadily to several striking viewpoints before it joins the Calypso Trail, near the summit.

**Calypso Trail** (moderate/1 km, one way): From the southwest end of the parking lot the Calypso Trail drops down to Millstream Creek and a picturesque ravine. Look for trillium in the spring. The route then passes a side path on the right that links with the parking lot and climbs via a series of switchbacks to the summit, close to the junction with the Auburn Trail.

The viewpoint at the Mill Hill summit (203 m) offers a magnificent vista of Victoria, the Highlands, Esquimalt Harbour plus the surrounding hills and seascapes.

**Worth Noting:**

- Mill Hill's lower forest consists mainly of western red cedar, Douglas-fir and hemlock. The summit is predominately Garry oak and arbutus. From April through June you will find the tiny calypso orchid or fairy slipper growing in the park's more forested, shady regions.
- Keep to designated trails and do not pick any flowers.
- A short trail leads from the parking lot to CRD Park Headquarters where you can pick up free CRD park brochures including, a checklist for Mill Hill's wildflowers, or make further inquiries.
- The summit cairn, built on the remains of an old forestry lookout tower, commemorates the CRD's 35th anniversary.

**Nearby:**
From the summit continue 1 km down Mill Hill's north side on the Calypso Trail to connect with Thetis Lake Park and with the Galloping Goose Trail via Six Mile Road.

Evidence of shell middens can be found in the park. Before European contact, the Songhees people camped along Millstream Creek. Later, the creek (also referred to as the Mill Stream and Rowe's Stream) supplied power for Vancouver Island's first sawmill. Located at Esquimalt Harbour, near Parson's Bridge, the mill was in operation as early as 1848.

*Columbine*

Photo: Di Chawner

## Flowers

What flower or tree is that? Enhance your walk or hike, take time to identify the fauna and flora around you. Carry your plant identification books with you, and take time to notice and identify the different plants along the trail.

*Swamp Lantern*

Photo: Joyce Folbigg

# Mount Wells

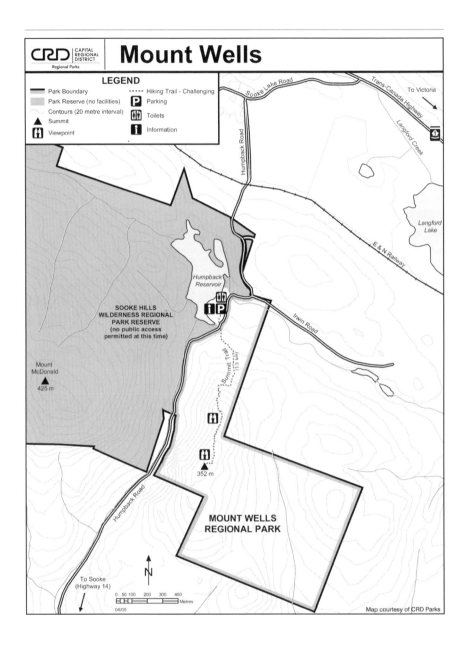

### LEGEND

- Park Boundary
- Park Reserve (no facilities)
- Contours (20 metre interval)
- ▲ Summit
- Viewpoint
- ⋯⋯ Hiking Trail - Challenging
- **P** Parking
- Toilets
- **i** Information

To Victoria

Langford Lake

Humpback Reservoir

SOOKE HILLS
WILDERNESS REGIONAL
PARK RESERVE
(no public access
permitted at this time)

Mount
McDonald
▲
425 m

Summit Trail
(1.3 km)

▲
352 m

MOUNT WELLS
REGIONAL PARK

To Sooke
(Highway 14)

N

0 50 100 200 300 400
Metres

04/05

Map courtesy of CRD Parks

## 20. Mount Wells

**Highlights:** A strenuous climb to the summit of Mount Wells Regional Park, in Langford, offers a striking view of Southern Vancouver Island, including Victoria, the Juan de Fuca Strait and the Sooke Hills. This fragile area explodes with spring wildflowers and there are excellent opportunities for wildlife viewing.

**Difficulty/Distance:** strenuous/1.3 km, one way

**Cautions:** In wet weather there will be muddy sections and slick rock so wear proper footwear.

Mount Wells is a wilderness area. Go properly prepared and carry adequate water for the steep ascent.

**Access:** From Victoria, take Highway #1 (Trans-Canada) to Sooke Lake Road and turn left. This signposted junction is also the turn for Goldstream Provincial Park's campground. Swing left on Humpback Road keep right at Irwin Road, and continue to the parking area, about 1.5 km from the start of Humpback Road. From Victoria, allow 30 minutes driving time. The park is open from sunrise to sunset.

**Hike Description:**
The CRD's **Mount Wells Regional Park** (123 ha) features a steep 1.3 km trail to the viewpoint at the Mount Wells summit (352 m). The route traverses patches of loose dirt in dry weather and open rock.

From the start on Humpback Road, the park's Summit Trail crosses an old water pipeline that once was a flow line out of the now disused Humpback Reservoir. The trail leaves the Douglas-fir forest of the lower regions and ascends through drier, open rocky terrain, where Garry oak, arbutus, hairy manzanita and delicate mosses grow. At the top your reward is a panoramic vista of Victoria, the Juan de Fuca Strait and the Sooke Hills, to the west.

**Worth Noting:**

- Spring wildflowers are abundant. Look for camas, satin flowers and shooting stars. The endangered prairie lupine grows in only one place in Canada, on Mount Wells. Stay on designated trails to protect the area's fragile vegetation and soil.

- Watch for Turkey Vultures riding overhead thermals. Listen for the drumming calls of blue grouse. The park is also habitat for deer, squirrels and alligator lizards. The latter are often spotted sunning themselves on rocks.

**Nearby:**
Sooke Hills Wilderness Regional Park Reserve (4100 ha) provides an undeveloped forest buffer zone for the Victoria area's water supply at Sooke Lake. Both this reserve and Mount Wells Regional Park are part of the Sea to Sea Green Blue Belt, protected forests that separate urban regions from the wilderness areas further west.

Photo: Di Chawner

*Lunch Break*

# 21. Metchosin Shoreline

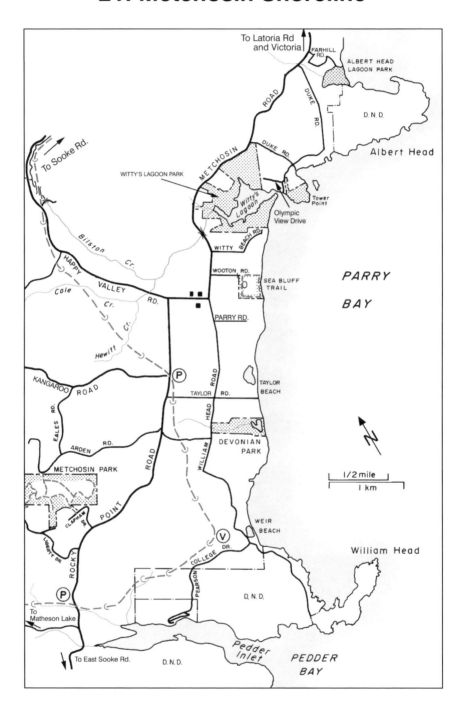

## 21. Metchosin Shoreline

**Highlights:** Metchosin features some of southern Vancouver Island's most picturesque hiking destinations. Popular trails at Albert Head, Witty's Lagoon, Sea Bluff Trail and Devonian parks lead through forests and grasslands to salt marshes, sandy beaches, quiet lagoons, rocky shorelines, seaside bluffs and breathtaking seascapes. The area is a mecca for birdwatchers and habitat for a variety of plants and animals.

**Difficulty/Distance:** easy to moderate/0.3 km to 1.7 km, one way

**Access**: From Victoria, follow Highway #1 (Trans-Canada) west. There are several options to access Metchosin Road. Either take Exit 10 (Colwood), travel through the business "strip" of View Royal and Colwood and follow Sooke Road to the Metchosin Road junction (take a left); or alternatively (and probably a little faster) from Victoria continue on Highway #1 and take Exit 14 through Langford on Veterans Memorial Parkway to its end at a rock face and T-junction. Turn left (Latoria Road) and continue to another T-junction. Turn right onto Metchosin Road.

### Albert Head Lagoon

**Access:** The first park is Albert Head Lagoon Regional Park. Take the next left off Metchosin Road onto Farhill Road, then make an immediate right turn onto Park Drive (lower) which becomes Delgada Road and leads to limited parking at the beach (gated in the evening). From Victoria, allow 30 minutes driving time. The park is open 7 am to sunset.

### Hike Description:

**Albert Head Lagoon Trail** (easy/0.3 km, one way): This small CRD park (7.1 ha) encircles a picture-perfect lagoon which is almost closed off by its gravel berm. A diversity of plants grow along the berm and the lagoon nature sanctuary is great for bird watching. Keep an eye out for mute swans, ducks, geese and other migrating waterfowl. There is a short stretch of cobble beach.

### Worth Noting:

In 1846, Captain Kellett named Albert Head after HRH Prince Albert, husband to Queen Victoria, because of its proximity to Victoria. Just north of the parking lot is the site of Vancouver Island's first steam-powered sawmills.

The next park along Metchosin Road is Witty's Lagoon.

## Witty's Lagoon

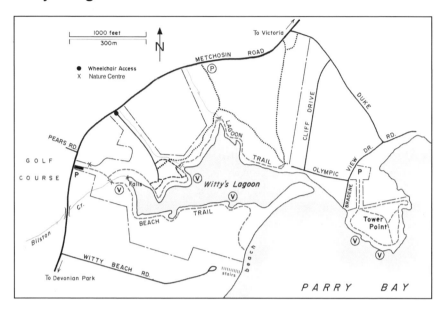

**Access to Tower Point:** For the Tower Point section of the park, continue from Farhill Road west on Metchosin Road, past Duke Road and Chapel Heights Drive to a second Duke Road junction. Turn left onto Duke Road, then right on to Olympic View Drive to the park entrance. (See map on page 98.) In winter, the limited grass parking area is closed so you must park on the road. Beyond the parking lot at the end of Bradene Road, off Olympic View Drive, there are steps down to the water. Tower Point facilities include toilets and a picnic area. From Victoria, allow 40 minutes driving time.

**Hike Description:**

**Tower Point** (easy/1.2 km loop): From the parking area on Olympic View Drive the gravel trail cuts through a bushy area to a large, grassy meadow. Several paths criss-cross the meadow. Continue along the shoreline trail. The pocket beaches on the point's west side are excellent places to study pillow basalt, formed about 55 million years ago when molten rock (magma) was cooled by ocean waters. Hike along the bluffs for a front-row view of harbour seals just off shore. Short, steep scrambles down the rocks lead to several tiny, rocky beaches.

**Worth Noting:**

At the end of Olympic View Drive, there are signposted hiking and equestrian trails leading to the main part of Witty's Lagoon Park. Use the Tower Point parking lot, as parking at this trail access is very limited.

**Main Access:** The main entrance to Witty's Lagoon is farther down Metchosin Road with the parking lot, small office and access trail across from the Metchosin Golf Club. This is the best parking area and the closest access to the Nature House and Sitting Lady Falls. Witty's Lagoon may also be reached by turning left off Metchosin Road at Witty Beach Road (with limited parking and long, steep steps down to a pleasant beach). One can hike between the beach, the waterfall and the Nature Centre. The Nature Centre, a picnic area and toilets are wheelchair accessible. From Victoria, allow 40 minutes driving time. The park is open 8 am to sunset.

**Hike Descriptions:**

 Metchosin's Witty's Lagoon Regional Park (57 ha) has over 5 km of trails to explore, including two which skirt the lagoon. Though not adjoining, a loop trail at Tower Point is also part of the park.

**Beach Trail** (moderate/1.5 km, one way): The Beach Trail is the most popular hike at Witty's Lagoon. The trail starts at the Nature Centre and leads down a sharp incline to a junction. (The path to the left is the Lagoon Trail, briefly described next.) The Beach Trail follows the right fork to the well-built bridge spanning Bilston Creek. Cross the creek to Sitting Lady Falls, a 50-m-high park highlight. There is a viewing platform here. The waterfall is spectacular in the winter and spring after heavy rains. The trail narrows as it begins its steepest descent to sea level and skirts the lagoon and its estuary salt marsh. Watch for Great Blue Herons foraging in shoreline shallows. A multitude of shorebirds and ducks frequent these protected waters.

The trail ends at the sandy beach on Parry Bay. At extreme low tide the beach and sandspit stretch out approximately 500 m in length. This is the best time to explore the many tidepools in the intertidal zone. Do not disturb or remove any marine life. At times of higher tides, watch for harbour seals in Parry Bay. The view from the beach includes Tower Point, the Haystock Islets, Race Rocks, Victoria and the seascapes across Juan de Fuca Strait.

**Lagoon Trail** (moderate/1.7 km, one way): From the trail junction near the Bilston Creek bridge the Lagoon Trail swings left and curves around the lagoon's north side to access the park service road and Whitney-Griffiths Point (picnic area, toilets and viewpoint). The trail continues east to Olympic View Road, which links to Tower Point.

**Worth Noting:**

- There are several bridle paths on Witty's Lagoon's north side.
- Please keep to marked trails to protect fragile vegetation.
- Witty's Lagoon is one place where cyclamen (the primrose family) grows wild.
- Tides permitting, a 3-km one-way hike from Witty's Lagoon to Taylor Road or Devonian Park is possible. The hike follows the shelving, pebble beach.
- For information on the park's Nature Centre hours, interpretive programs and wheelchair access, contact CRD Parks. (See page 167.) A pamphlet is available detailing over 160 species of birds seen at Witty's Lagoon.

Witty's Lagoon was the site of the village of the Ka-Kyaakan band in the 1850s when the first settlers arrived. Through the Douglas Treaties the Hudson's Bay Company purchased Metchosin from the band for the equivalent in blankets of under 44 British pounds. The village was abandoned in the early 1860s. The few surviving members, practiced in Songhees ways and traditions, moved to Esquimalt to join the main Songhees tribe. The park is named after John Witty, a neighbouring landowner from 1867 on.

**Sea Bluff Trail**
**Access:** Next along Metchosin Road is Wooton Road, on the left, which leads to Sea Bluff Trail. The trail is accessed from Wooton Road and also from Parry Road (off William Head Road) and Parry Cross Road. Parking is very limited. From Victoria allow 45 minutes driving time.

**Hike Description:**
**Sea Bluff Trail:** (easy/1.2 km loop): Sea Bluff Trail winds around open fields, through woods and past an irrigation pond. Sea views along the 50-m-high bluffs look south across Parry Bay to William Head and the Olympic Mountains. Only the perimeter trail is public access. The open space in the centre is part of an operating farm. Please do not hike over this area and do not disturb the sheep. Dogs MUST be leashed at all times, and keep the gate closed. Public access depends on this.

**Worth Noting:**
Geoff and Jacqueline Mitchell, long-time Metchosin residents, donated the property for the Sea Bluff Trail.

**Devonian Park**

**Access:** For Devonian, the final shoreline park in the series, continue on Metchosin Road past Metchosin town centre (where Metchosin Road becomes William Head Road) to Devonian Park. The picnic area and toilets near the parking area are wheelchair accessible. From Victoria, allow 45 minutes driving time. The park is open sunrise to sunset.

**Hike Description:**

**Beach Trail, Devonian Park** (moderate/0.9 km, one way): This trail at the CRD's Devonian Regional Park (14 ha) winds through a shady Douglas-fir and bigleaf maple forest carpeted in a lush, seasonal growth of ferns. The route twists and turns along Sherwood Creek (there are a few steep sections) to emerge at a cobble beach on Parry Bay. Here you will find an impressive view of Race Rocks, the Olympic Mountains and Juan de Fuca Strait. You might even spot a pod of orcas gliding by. Sherwood Pond is a year round birdwatcher's delight.

**Worth Noting:**

- The Helgesen bridle trail contours down to the beach along the park's western boundary.
- Captain Kellett of HMS *Herald* named Parry Bay and William Head after his friend, the noted Arctic explorer, Rear Admiral Sir William Edward Parry.

**Nearby:**

There are many other municipal parks, trails and green space corridors in Metchosin. (See the Western Metchosin section on page 105.)

---

Sherwood Pond used to be one of many lagoons found along the Metchosin coast. Its barrier spit eventually closed off the lagoon, leaving it, and a population of sea-run cutthroat trout, landlocked. Usually trout fry leave for the ocean in their second or third year and return to spawn in their fourth. This population adapted to fresh water for life. The cobble barrier is porous enough to allow some water passage, so the level of the pond can vary by as much as two metres.

---

# 22. Western Metchosin

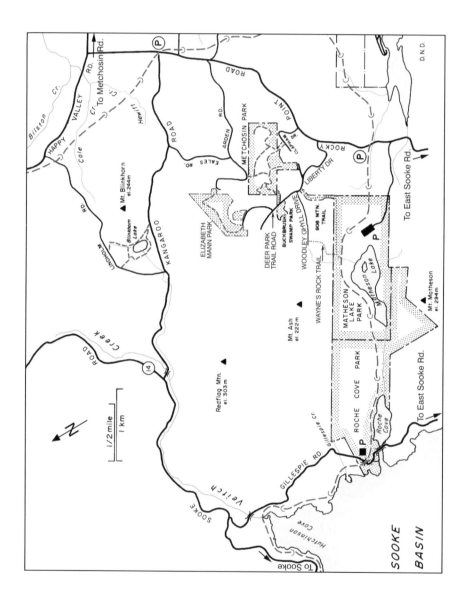

## 22. Western Metchosin

**Highlights:** Metchosin has many delightful parks and trails including some of the prettiest parts of the Galloping Goose Trail. Matheson Lake Regional Park (157 ha) features a loop trail that circles the lake and provides opportunities for hiking, nature appreciation and wildlife viewing. Roche Cove Regional Park (163 ha) offers over seven kilometres of hiking trails, to enjoy the beauty and seclusion of the cove. There are ocean and hilltop viewpoints and the forests harbour groves of large old-growth cedars. Metchosin's lesser-known rural hiking trails and parks are all worth exploring.

**Difficulty/Distance:** easy to strenuous/varies

**Cautions:** Mosquitoes can be problematic in low-lying regions.

In wet weather, or just after, trails near lakes, creeks and boggy areas can become extremely muddy and slippery.

### Matheson Lake

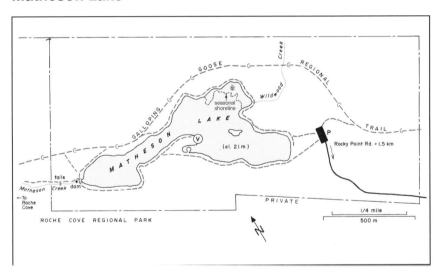

**Access:** Follow Highway #1 (Trans-Canada) west from Victoria and take Exit 14 to Langford. Drive south on Veterans Memorial Parkway to Sooke Road. Turn right and head west towards Sooke. From Sooke Road turn left on Happy Valley Road, then right on Rocky Point Road and right again onto Matheson Lake Park Road to the parking lot. From Victoria, allow 35 minutes driving time. This CRD park is open sunrise to sunset.

**Hike Description:**

**Matheson Lake Loop** (moderate/3.4 km loop): Start from the beach and picnic area, a short walk from the parking lot, with Matheson Lake on your left. Hike the trail to Wildwood Creek and continue around the lake's north side. Be prepared for some up and down hiking. Avoid any trails on the right that lead away from the lake. At the junction with the Galloping Goose Trail, watch for cyclists and equestrians.

At Matheson Lake's west end, cross Matheson Creek on a bridge near an old dam and backtrack east to our starting point. The seasonal trail west along Matheson Creek passes a waterfall and roughly parallels the Galloping Goose Trail to Roche Cove. (See page 108.) About halfway along the lake's south side take the side trail to a small point of land and lake viewpoint.

**Worth Noting:**

- Western red cedar and Douglas-fir dominate the low-lying forest. You can identify lodgepole pines on the rocky outcrops. Willow and dogwood prefer areas near the lakeshore. In the spring, listen and watch for woodpeckers.

- Matheson Lake is a popular swimming, angling and canoeing destination.

- Bicycles and horses are restricted to the Galloping Goose Trail.

**Nearby:**

The Galloping Goose Trail intersects the park and connects with Roche Cove Regional Park. From the Galloping Goose at Wildwood Creek a trail leads up to Wayne's Rock and accesses the steep Bob Mountain Park Trail, and other district trails. (See page 109.)

---

The trail along the creek from Matheson Lake to Roche Cove was an oldtimers' portage trail in the 1850s and '60s. Part of the Lake Pass and Barde Knockie Trail, the route extended from Sooke to Bilston Farm and on to Victoria.

---

# Roche Cove

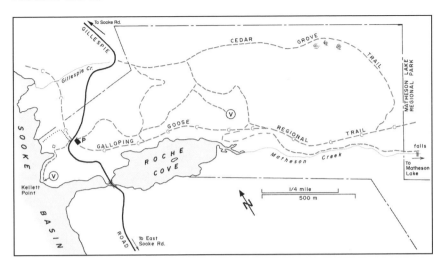

**Access**: From Victoria follow Highway #1 (Trans-Canada) and take Exit 14 to Langford. Drive south on Veterans Memorial Parkway to Sooke Road. Turn right and head west towards Sooke. Near the 17 Mile House, turn left onto Gillespie Road and continue another 3 km to the parking lot. From Victoria, allow 45 minutes driving time. This CRD park is open sunrise to sunset. The Roche Cove parking lot toilets are wheelchair accessible.

**Cautions:** Low-lying areas may be wet, muddy and seasonally impassable. On the Matheson Creek Trail beware of protruding roots. This trail is steepest nearer Matheson Lake.

### Hike Descriptions:
Several hiking trails begin near the Roche Cove parking area. You can combine some of these with the Galloping Goose Trail to create your own loop hike. It is a short walk to the park's small picnic area and a pocket beach on Roche Cove.

**Galloping Goose Trail** (easy/4.5 km to Matheson Lake, one way): Take the Galloping Goose east to Matheson Lake along a relatively flat, wide, gravel trail. As you travel through the old railway rock cuts, look for the splashy yellow flowers of stonecrop, a succulent that blooms in the late spring. Near the 34-km marker, a short, steep side trail (which also links with the Matheson Creek Trail to Matheson Lake) descends to the head of Roche Cove. This protected cove, near the mouth of Matheson Creek, has a tidal mud flat beach and rocky shoreline.

**Cedar Grove Trail** (moderate/1.9 km, one way): At the north end of the parking area the trail winds uphill past mossy rock outcrops and through a forest of large bigleaf maple trees. Follow the Cedar Grove Trail signposts. There are confusing junctions and cross paths on the way. One marked trail goes to a former viewpoint, now obscured by trees.

Swing east at a major fork to a grove of cedars. A few trees here are over 500 years old. Continue east to pass an alder forest on the left. This is a good birdwatching area in the spring or fall. The trail, now less distinct, eventually drops down to the Galloping Goose Trail, near Matheson Lake Regional Park's western boundary. Take the Galloping Goose back to the starting point. Just before the parking lot is a great view of Roche Cove.

**Matheson Creek Trail** (moderate/seasonal): From the parking area follow the Galloping Goose Trail to Roche Cove's east end (near the 34-km marker) and the start of a seasonal trail to Matheson Lake. High water may render the route impassable in the winter. There are two creek crossings (one on stones, the other on a log) and some changes in elevation. Watch your step carefully.

The bracken fern is profuse in this temperate rainforest. One highlight is a grove of western red cedars. Maintain a stealthy pace through the low-lying, often muddy areas. You will have a better chance of catching a fleeting glimpse of a salamander, particularly near rotten logs.

**Kellett Point** (easy/150 m, one way): On the west side of Gillespie Road a trail leads to Kellett Point, three tiny beaches, lovely grassy slopes and beautiful views of Sooke Basin and the Olympic Mountains. Kellett Point is an excellent picnic area.

**Worth Noting:**

- Watch for Belted Kingfishers and river otters at Kellett Point and Roche Cove.
- Migrating ducks and shorebirds frequent area waters in the early spring and late summer.
- Bicycles and horses are restricted to the Galloping Goose Trail.

**Nearby:**
Matheson Lake is directly east of Roche Cove. The Galloping Goose Trail intersects both regional parks.

Roche Cove (and Roche Harbour, San Juan Island, USA) are named after Richard Roche (later Captain), RN, who served as midshipman under Captain Henry Kellett (for whom Kellett Point is named) aboard the *Herald*. In 1845, Captain Kellett first had to take the *Herald* to the Arctic in search of Sir John Franklin before undertaking a survey of Victoria and Esquimalt harbours and Sooke Inlet, a year later. Roche also served as mate (again with Captain Kellett) on the Arctic exploring ship *Resolute*, 1852-54.

## Blinkhorn Lake

**Access:** From Victoria proceed as for Matheson Lake to Sooke Road. Head west on Highway #14 (Sooke Road) and turn left on Kangaroo Road. Continue a little past Lindholm Road and watch for the trailhead, on the left. There is very little roadside parking.

## Hike Description:

Blinkhorn Lake Nature Park (18.2 ha) is a pleasant spot to visit, with a woodland trail encircling a picturesque lake and lowland. There are opportunities for birdwatching and nature appreciation. Side trails lead to Lindholm Road trailheads.

## Worth Noting:

- Blinkhorn Lake Nature Park is located on land acquired from the Greater Victoria Water District in 1999.

Blinkhorn Lake and mountain are named after Thomas Blinkhorn. He and his wife, Anne, arrived in 1851 as independent settlers to manage Captain James Cooper's Metchosin farm. Years earlier, as a stockman in Australia, Blinkhorn had rescued Captain Sir John Franklin, lost in the bush. Thomas Blinkhorn served as magistrate from 1853 to his death in 1856.

## Metchosin Wilderness Park, Buckbrush Swamp, Elizabeth Mann Park, Bob Mountain Trail and Wayne's Rock Trail

**Cautions:** Roadside parking is very limited at most trailheads. The best place to park is at either of two designated Galloping Goose Trail lots: one at the junction of Rocky Point and Kangaroo roads; the other farther along Rocky Point Road, about 4 km past Kangaroo Road. From these CRD parking lots you can walk to several area trailheads. (See page 104.)

**Access**: Follow Highway #1 (Trans-Canada) west from Victoria and take Exit 14 to Langford. Drive south on Veterans Memorial Parkway to Sooke Road. Turn right and head west towards Sooke. From Sooke Road (Highway 14) turn left on Happy Valley Road, then right on Rocky Point Road to the signposted Galloping Goose parking lots. From Victoria, allow 35 minutes driving time. The trails are open sunrise to sunset.

**Hike Descriptions:**

**Metchosin Wilderness Park** (40.5 ha): This park is situated between Arden Road and Clapham Drive and is also known as Hundred Acre Park. On a hot day the park is an excellent destination for a cool, shady hike. There are quiet woods, small creeks and great opportunities for nature appreciation and birdwatching. Trailheads are located on Liberty Drive, Deer Park Trail Road, Arden Road and at the main signposted entrance on Clapham Drive. Various corridors and bridle paths link the park with Elizabeth Mann Park and neighbourhood trails.

**From the Clapham Road** entrance (limited roadside parking) follow the main trail through a stand of alders. At a major trail junction, bear left, cross a wooden bridge and hike west through the park to Liberty Drive, directly opposite the Buckbrush Swamp Trail. Or turn right at the junction on a 3-km circular hike that winds through the deep forest and around marshland.

In the shadows of tall western red cedars, gigantic sword fern thrive on the forest floor. You will also see bracken fern, salal and ocean spray. Thickets pervade around the marsh and in the spring, its east end is rife with swamp lantern (skunk cabbage). Part of the loop trail traverses drier terrain where the forest has more Douglas-fir mixed in with the cedars and Oregon grape mingles with trailside salal.

**Buckbrush Swamp Trail**: The trailhead is located on Liberty Drive. Trails link with Metchosin Wilderness Park. An easy, signposted loop trail circles Buckbrush Swamp and provides opportunities for wetland observation and birdwatching.

**Elizabeth Mann Park** (17 ha): Trailheads are located on Arden Road and Deer Park Trail Road. Trails connect to Metchosin Wilderness Park. The steep trail to a viewpoint off Deer Park Trail Road is for hiking only. A variety of forested hiking trails and bridle paths snake through the park.

**Bob Mountain Trail:** The north end trailhead is on Liberty Drive, near Woodley Ghyll Drive. Located within Bob Mountain Park (1.3 ha), the Bob Mountain links Metchosin Wilderness Park with the Galloping Goose Trail, near Matheson Lake. The Bob Mountain Trail is steep and strenuous.

It meanders along the narrow park corridor south to Matheson Lake Park's northern boundary, turns west and then descends south to the Galloping Goose Trail. Expect numerous confusing side paths and places where the route is indistinct.

**Wayne's Rock Trail:** Access is off Woodley Ghyll Drive. The trail runs south to Matheson Lake Park and connects with the Galloping Goose Trail, just east of Wildwood Creek.

**Worth Noting:**

- Many unmarked old roads, bridle paths and side trails lead to private property. Please stay on the main routes and do not trespass.
- Equestrians share many area trails. Be courteous to all trail-users.
- Cycling is only permitted on the Galloping Goose Trail.
- For more information on Metchosin trails contact: district.metchosin.bc.ca.

**Nearby:**
Four Metchosin shoreline parks along Metchosin Road (Albert Head, Witty's Lagoon, Sea Bluff Trail and Devonian) are close by. (See page 98.) The Galloping Goose Trail intersects the region and is accessed at several points, notably along Rocky Point Road and at Matheson Lake Park.

Metchosin so far has managed to retain its rural charm for the enjoyment of residents and visitors alike. Be sure to visit the historic Metchosin School, dating back to 1871 and one of Canada's first public schools. It is located on Happy Valley Road, across from the Municipal Hall. The museum is open weekend afternoons in the spring, summer and fall. Contact the Municipal Hall for information. Another nearby stop of interest is St. Mary's Church, consecrated in 1873. In the spring, Easter lilies surround the church building with a vision of white blooms.

# 23. East Sooke

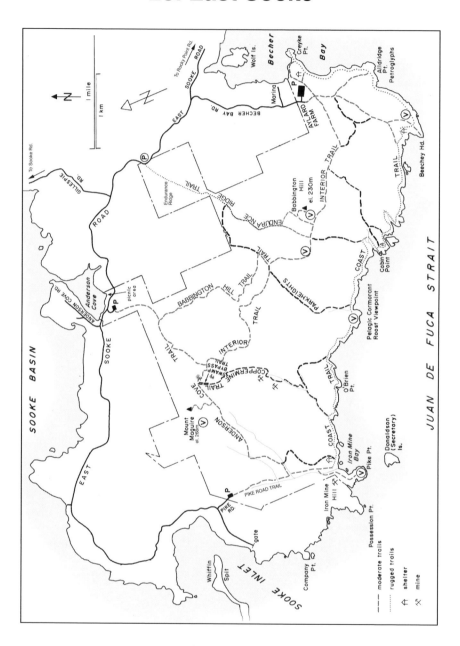

## 23. East Sooke

**Highlights:** The CRD's East Sooke Regional Park (1435 ha) is a hiker's paradise. The park has 50 km of spectacular wilderness trails that offer a diversity of day hikes from short walks to longer, more challenging treks. Many trails intersect so you can create your own loop hike. East Sooke Park features breathtaking seascapes, dense rainforests, panoramic mountain viewpoints and superlative opportunities for wildlife viewing, birdwatching and nature appreciation.

**Difficulty/Distance:** easy to strenuous/400 m to 10 km and up, one way

**Cautions:** The Mount Maguire routes cross rough terrain and may not be suitable for children. Expect a lot of laborious up-and-down hiking. The hills get steeper the higher you climb.

Much of the Coast Trail traverses rocky ground and is sometimes hard to locate. If you become momentarily disoriented, to regain your bearings, simply backtrack until you locate a Coast Trail indicator (yellow markers on rocks), which shows the designated route. In general, avoid any inland paths and keep to the coast.

Carry good maps (consider a topographical chart) and check the park information boards closely. Familiarize yourself with your planned destination prior to your hike. GPS units and cell phones may not work in all parts of the park.

Never hike alone and allow ample time for a return journey. If hiking the complete Coast Trail consider leaving a second vehicle at your destination parking lot or arrange for a ride back to your starting point.

Most park trails are uneven and rocky. Expect protruding roots, loose rocks and steep sections. Wear adequate footwear and dress warmly. Chilling sea breezes, sea fog and strong winds are prevalent along the coast. Prepare for capricious weather.

When hiking in coastal areas beware of dangerous rogue waves. Use extreme caution along cliff edges, bluffs and open rock faces.

Low-lying sections of the inland trails may flood over the winter.

Do not rely on creeks. Carry an adequate supply of water.

**Access:** East Sooke Park has three designated parking lots: Aylard Farm, Anderson Cove and Pike Road. From Victoria, allow approximately an hour's driving time. The park is open 8 am to sunset. At Aylard Farm the trail, beach approach and toilets are wheelchair accessible.

**Access to Aylard Farm:** Follow Highway #1 (Trans-Canada) west from Victoria and take Exit 14 to Langford. Drive south on Veterans Memorial Parkway to Sooke Road. Turn right and head west towards Sooke. Turn left onto Gillespie Road to East Sooke Road. Make a left onto East Sooke Road and right on Becher Bay Road to the park entrance.

**Hike Descriptions:**

**Aylard Farm to Becher Bay** (easy/400 m, one way): With nearby park facilities (picnic sites, toilets), good access to sandy beaches and other hiking options, Aylard Farm is a popular destination for a family outing. A short 10-minute hike from the parking lot leads through the remains of old apple orchards and open meadows to the sandy Becher Bay beach. A set of stairs drops down to the beach. From here take a side trip to the Creyke Point lookout (with a view of the coast from Metchosin to Victoria) and the strange rock formations at the headland. From Aylard Farm you can follow the Interior Trail to access Babbington Hill (230 m). The steep route to the summit is tiring but worth the effort. The view across Juan de Fuca Strait to the Olympic Mountains is spectacular.

**Aylard Farm to Beechey Head** (moderate/3 km, one way): From the parking area, hike through the old Aylard farm site to Becher Bay. Turn right and follow the Coast Trail for about 30 minutes to Alldridge Point, which features Coast Salish petroglyphs and was designated a Provincial Heritage Site in 1927. At this point take a shortcut inland trail back to Aylard Farm or continue along the coast to Beechey Head, a popular fishing spot and excellent viewpoint. This headland is one of the best places on southern Vancouver Island to observe the annual "Hawk Watch" or Turkey Vulture migration. (See page 117.) Retrace your steps along the coast or return to the parking lot on the slightly shorter inland trail.

**Access to Anderson Cove:** As per Aylard Farm access to East Sooke Road. Turn right onto East Sooke road to the parking area, on the left. A beautiful picnic site (with toilets) is located across the road on Anderson Cove.

**Hike Description:**

**Mount Maguire via the Anderson Cove Trail** (moderate to strenuous/3 to 3.5 km, one way): Begin your hike up Mount Maguire from either the Pike Road or Anderson Cove trailheads. Both signposted routes lead to the Mount Maguire summit trail, but the Pike Road access is slightly shorter.

From Anderson Cove the trail negotiates a steep grade and follows a meandering southwest course through the shady forest. There are links to several of the park's less-travelled inland connectors, including the

Babbington Hill and the Interior trails. Near a swampy area you will reach the junction with the Coppermine Trail. A little south down the Coppermine Trail are some old mine workings.

Keep west along the Anderson Cove Trail and soon you will reach the marked turnoff for Mount Maguire. Swing north for the summit. The short but strenuous final pitch to the top includes a dried-up creekbed with loose rock, which may be slippery. Open rock faces turn dangerously slick in wet weather. The viewpoint at the Mount Maguire summit (268 m) takes in the surrounding hills, Juan de Fuca Strait, the Olympic Peninsula, Donaldson Island, Iron Mine Bay and Possession Point.

**Access to Pike Road:** As per Aylard Farm access to East Sooke Road. Swing right at East Sooke Road, drive past Anderson Cove and turn left onto Pike Road to one of two small parking areas.

**Hike Descriptions:**

**Pike Road Trail** (easy/1.2 km, one way): From the parking lot head south on the level path of an old logging road. Part way to the coast, the Anderson Cove Trail comes in on the left, near Pike Creek. This is the cutoff for Mount Maguire, for those hiking in from the west. Turn left onto the Anderson Cove Trail and continue east to the Mount Maguire cutoff. (See description above.)

The Pike Road Trail makes a short descent as it nears the sea. Just before Iron Mine Bay, a trail on the right leads past old mine workings to a viewpoint at Pike Point, a small isthmus of land that juts out into the strait. The bay's name is a reminder of the iron and copper mining enterprises that operated in the area between 1863 and 1971.

Iron Mine Bay features a beautiful pebble beach and views of the bay, Juan de Fuca Strait, Donaldson (Secretary) Island and Pike Point. At low tide, explore the intertidal zones at Iron Mine Bay. You will discover a myriad of marine life and seaweeds. A small shelter is located above Iron Mine Bay at the west end of the Coast Trail.

**Coast Trail** (strenuous/10 km, one way): The most challenging trail at East Sooke Park is the 10 km route from Iron Mine Bay to Aylard Farm. Recommended for energetic hikers only, the trail has magnificent seascapes, views of the Olympic Peninsula, secluded coves and bays, cliffs, rocky bluffs, seaside chasms, deep ravines and an atmosphere of remoteness and adventure.

Start at either end of the Coast Trail, but the CRD recommends you begin at the Pike Road trailhead and travel east to Aylard Farm. From the parking lot take the wide Pike Road Trail south to Iron Mine Bay. Turn east to follow the Coast Trail signpost. The first trail junction you reach, on the left, loops north to the Anderson Cove Trail. Near O'Brien Point you can choose from two trails that branch off onto the Coppermine Trail.

Halfway down the Coast Trail, where sharp, jagged cliffs thrust up from the waters of the strait, pelagic cormorants roost along the rocky bluffs. The birds are often seen diving for food. The Parkheights Trail junction is close by. Near Cabin Point several paths swing inland to join the Interior Trail in the vicinity of Babbington Hill. A particularly confusing section is on the descent from the bluffs as you approach Cabin Point. Here, near an open area just before the headland, watch closely for the correct turn, to the right, where the trail drops into a steep gully. Avoid the false trail straight ahead.

The restored Trap Shack near Cabin Point dates back to the early 1900s and is testimony to East Sooke's rich fishing history. Take the time to explore the wide pebble beach on the nearby shallow bay. This sheltered cove is a great choice for a rest stop. Continue east along the rugged coastline bluffs toward Beechey Head. The lookout is a popular place during the annual hawk migration (See page 117.) From Beechey Head you can take one of two inland paths to Aylard Farm or keep along the coast via Alldridge Point.

**Endurance Ridge Trail** (strenuous/2.9 km, one way): Along the west side of East Sooke Road (between Becher Bay Road and Gillespie Road and close to Seedtree Road) watch for a small roadside parking area. This is the trailhead for the Endurance Ridge Trail, a rough alternate route to Babbington Hill and Cabin Point. It starts with a long, grueling 2.9 km climb up Endurance Ridge. The trail runs southwest to connect with the routes to Babbington Hill, the Interior Trail and the Coast Trail, near Cabin Point.

**Worth Noting:**

- Please do not disturb or remove any plants, animals or marine life.
- Bicycles are not permitted on East Sooke Park trails.

**Nearby:**
Roche Cove and the Galloping Goose Trail are situated just to the north-east, off Gillespie Road. (See pages 107 and 148.)

In the spring and summer, flower enthusiasts may find a variety of species. Look for Indian paintbrush, fringe cup, orange honeysuckle, patches of stonecrop, monkey flower, hardtack, white clover, harvest brodiaea, white campion, blue camas, death camas, western buttercup, red columbine, small-flower alumroot, white clover, Queen Anne's lace, seaside woolly sunflower, hedge nettle, cluster white rose, fairy orchids, red elderberry, sea blush, Columbia tiger lily, nodding onion, white triteleia and mullein and many more.

~ ~ ~

Beechey Head is a prime spot to witness the annual fall Turkey Vulture migration or "Hawk Watch". Each year, hundreds of these birds gather overhead, in final staging prior to their lengthy crossing of Juan de Fuca Strait. The migration starts in mid-September and runs through the end of October, peaking around the end of September. For best viewing, choose a sunny, warm day, in the late morning to early afternoon. That's when there are scores of birds wheeling and soaring high up in the daily thermals. As well as the Turkey Vultures, try to identify other raptors like Red-tailed Hawks, Merlin, Cooper's Hawks, Bald Eagles, Peregrine Falcons, Ospreys and American Kestrels.

Hiking distances at East Sooke Park can be deceptive because of rough terrain and the surprising amount of up and down travel. Many trail intersections, overgrown old roads, side paths and game trails are unmarked and confusing. It is wise to begin your hike early in the day and not overestimate your capabilities. Always allow more than enough time to return to your vehicle before dark.

The major interconnecting trails are all well cut and signposted at key junctions. It is possible to shorten a hike and use one of these trails to return early, if necessary. Our map depicts officially signposted trails. Stick to the marked routes; more than one hiker has unintentionally spent an unexpected night in East Sooke Park.

Approximate minimum hiking times in East Sooke Park, one way:

Coast Trail (Iron Mine Bay to Aylard Farm, including Pike Road Trail) 6.5 to 7.5 hours, plus

| | |
|---|---|
| Aylard Farm to Beechey Head (via coast) | 1 hour |
| Aylard Farm to Beechey Head (via inland trail) | 45 minutes |
| Aylard Farm to Babbington Hill | 1 hour, 15 minutes |
| Beechey Head to Cabin Point | 1.5 to 2 hours |
| Cabin Point to Iron Mine Bay | 3.5 to 4 hours |
| Coppermine Trail to Interior Trail (from coast) | 1 hour |
| Parkheights Trail to Interior Trail (from coast) | 30 minutes |
| Pike Road to Iron Mine Bay | 30 minutes |
| Pike Road to Mount Maguire | 1.5 hours |
| Anderson Cove to Mount Maguire | 2 hours |
| Anderson Cove to Babbington Hill | 2 hours |
| Anderson Cove to Pike Road, via the Anderson Cove Trail | 2 hours |
| Interior Trail, from Anderson Cove Trail to Parkheights Trail | 1 hour, 15 minutes |
| Interior Trail, from Anderson Cove Trail to Aylard Farm | 3 hours |
| Endurance Ridge to Babbington Hill | 1.5 to 2 hours |

East Sooke Park's flora and fauna is as diverse as the nature of its trails. The woodland floor in the shady, dense lowland forest (Douglas-fir, western red cedar, alder and hemlock, with Sitka spruce closer to the coast) is carpeted with a variety of ferns. swamp lanterns (skunk cabbage) and fungi flourish in the wetter areas. The drier, upland forests are mainly comprised of arbutus, Garry oak, hairy manzanita and lodgepole pine. Near the windswept coast, the ubiquitous salal thrives alongside kinnikinnick and Oregon grape, despite a constant barrage from high winds and sea spray.

The park is home to resident and migratory birds, raccoons, squirrels, grouse, black-tail deer, pine martens, mink and the occasional cougar and black bear. Offshore you may spot seals, sea lions and river otters. Killer whales are common from the middle of May through September. Watch for gray whales February to April.

# 24. Whiffin Spit

Photo: Aldyth Hunter

## 24. Whiffin Spit

**Highlights:** Whiffin Spit Park is a beautiful sandy breakwater that separates Sooke Harbour and the Juan de Fuca Strait. A seaside trail to the end of the spit rewards hikers with striking seascapes and mountain vistas. Winter birdwatching is popular here and there are opportunities to view marine mammals and intertidal marine life.

**Difficulty/Distance:** easy/1.2 km, one way

**Cautions:** Dress warmly. The spit can be windy, the weather changeable.

**Access:** From Victoria, take Highway #1 (Trans-Canada) west to Exit 14, (Langford). Turn left on Veterans Memorial Parkway, continue south to Sooke Road and turn right. From the traffic lights in Sooke (at the junction of Otter Point Road and West Coast Road (#14), travel west another 1.8 km on West Coast Road to Whiffin Spit Road. Turn left and continue all the way to the beach and the parking area. From Victoria, allow 45 minutes driving time.

**Hike Description:**

The 1.2-km trail along Whiffin Spit begins at the parking lot at the end of Whiffin Spit Road. It is a pleasant 25-minute hike, past sand and gravel beaches and grassy areas, to the east end of the winding spit. One narrow section is only nine metres wide. Along the way are majestic views of Sooke, the Sooke Hills, the Juan de Fuca Strait and the Olympic Mountains. An added bonus is the chance to observe the reversing tidal currents near the marine navigation light at the end of Whiffin Spit. Time your hike for lower tides and follow the trail one way and, on your way back, beachcomb along the shoreline.

**Worth Noting:**

- Whiffin Spit, with its sandy shoreline and adjacent shallow waters, is an excellent destination for winter birdwatching (October to April). Among the shorebirds and migrant species to watch for are loons, scoters (diving ducks) and Western Grebes.

- Flocks of seagulls congregate in the offshore waters. Sightings may include Bonaparte's, Hermann's, Glaucous-winged and California gulls.

- Scan the skies for eagles and Turkey Vultures; the waters for otters and harbour seals.

- The spit is a popular dog-walking area.

Whiffin Spit extends out into Sooke Inlet and provides a semi-natural barrier that protects Sooke Harbour from the often turbulent sea conditions out on more exposed waters. The spit has been reinforced at a couple of breach points to allow continued access to the spit's east end.

~ ~ ~

Whiffin Spit is named after John George Whiffin, a clerk aboard the Royal Navy vessel Herald. The spit is situated beside Quimper Park, a heritage site commemorating the 1790 arrival of the first European ship in Sooke waters. In 1855, at this site, the pioneer Muir brothers operated the first successful steam sawmill in the Sooke area, using the boiler from a wrecked vessel. They were also shipbuilders.

**Nearby:**
The Sooke Potholes, the Galloping Goose Trail and other Sooke area hiking destinations are close to Whiffin Spit. (See pages 124 and 146.)

**Dog Guidelines**
In all the parks dogs are required to be leashed for the protection of the environment and for public safety.

**Bald Eagles, Turkey Vultures and Ospreys**

A mature Bald Eagle has a dark body, white head and white tail. It soars and glides with flat outstretched wings.

The Turkey Vulture is almost uniformly black. It soars with an unsteady, rocking motion, wings upturned in a distinctive U-shape or dihedral.

The Osprey has a white head with a dark eye-stripe, a clear white belly and its wings are light on the undersides, but dark on the topside. It flies and soars with wings held in the shape of a flattish letter "M".

For more information on these magnificent birds, see page 129.

# 25. Sooke Potholes

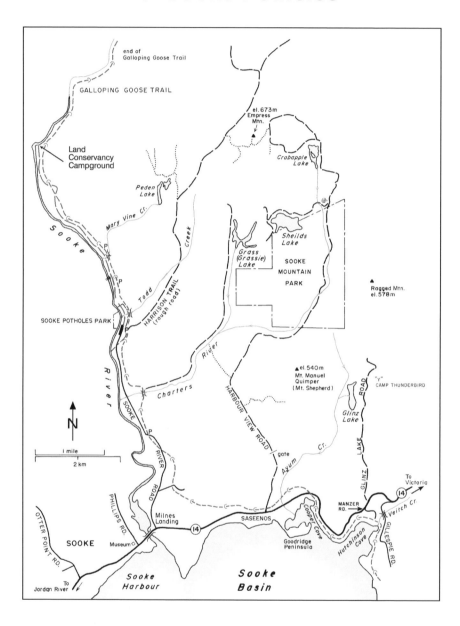

# 25. Sooke Potholes

**Highlights:** Created in 2005, in joint partnership with The Land Conservancy of British Columbia, the CRD's Sooke Potholes Regional Park (63.5 ha) is a must-see. The park protects a 5-km corridor along the Sooke River's eastern banks and ensures public access to the spectacular upper canyon, river potholes and pocket beaches. Trails lead upriver to several bluff viewpoints.

**Difficulty/Distance:** moderate/up to 5 km, one way

**Cautions:** Avoid the cliff edges.

After periods of heavy rain and in the off-season, beware of suddenly rising or falling water levels in the Sooke River. Dangerous, steep cliffs border the Sooke River. Wear proper footwear, exercise extreme caution near slippery rock surfaces and stay away from the drop-offs. Be particularly attentive with children.

**Access:** From Victoria, follow Highway #1 (Trans-Canada) and take Exit 14 to Langford. Drive south on Veterans Memorial Parkway to Sooke Road. Turn right and head west towards Sooke. Just before the Sooke River bridge, turn right onto Sooke River Road and continue north, about 6 km, to the park and the first of two parking lots.

The first parking lot is the Sooke Potholes Provincial Park. There is no hiking at this location. This park provides good access to swimming pools just to the north and inside the regional park. From Victoria, allow 45 minutes travel time.

To enter the regional park, drive north and turn right to The Land Conservancy information kiosk and small parking lot. This is where the main lodge of the failed Deertrail development once stood. You can follow short groomed trails to high bluffs that overlook the river canyon. Chain link fencing at these lookouts assures visitors a safe look at some dazzling green pools. Continue north to Parking Lot 2, where pay parking is in effect from May 1 to September 30. Contact CRD Parks for current information. (See page 167.)

## Hike Description:

The majority of park trails are largely undeveloped but a number of well-defined routes wander 5 km up the Sooke River Valley. There are short trails going down to the river at various points, often with steep sections closer to the river. Avoid cliff edges. Follow the road for a gentler grade, but remember cars will be travelling on this road as well.

Highlights are the river canyons, gorges, waterfalls, rapids, pocket beaches and potholes.

The Galloping Goose Regional Trail runs parallel to the park and provides a nice alternate hiking route. Watch for bicycles on this route and possibly horses.

**Worth Noting:**

- The Land Conservancy operates a seasonal campground on 8.5 ha of land at the park's north end. Contact: conservancy.bc.ca for more information. Camping and fires are prohibited elsewhere.

- Sooke Potholes Regional Park abuts the Sea to Sea Green Blue Belt (1628 ha), a CRD Regional Park Reserve that connects many protected wilderness areas. The reserve stretches from Saanich Inlet to the Sooke Basin.

**Nearby:**

**Sooke Mountain Provincial Park** (435 ha) is part of an extensive wilderness corridor preserving wildlife habitat and fragile watersheds. The park has been a backwoods recreation area since its creation in 1928. This part of the Sooke Hills is home to black bear, Vancouver Island gray wolf, cougar, Roosevelt elk and blacktail deer. You may hear grouse, red squirrels or even owls. For further information and map, contact BC Parks. (See page 167.)

**Cautions:** This is a back country park with no facilities. There is walk-in access only, which involves strenuous hiking in a remote area. There are no maintained hiking trails. Carry appropriate maps, compass and/or GPS unit. Be prepared for all kinds of weather. You may encounter bear or cougar. Fire closures may apply.

**Access:** From Harbour View Road, off Sooke Road, limited parking is available at the turnaround near the locked gate. Public entry over adjacent private lands has always been a contentious issue. Obey all posted notices and do not trespass.

From Sooke River Road, there are two back ways into the region. At Charters Creek, take the old road along Charters Creek and climb up to Grass (Grassie) Lake's west end. The Harrison Trail, a rough, overgrown old road off Sooke River Road, south of Todd Creek, provides trail access to Peden Lake and to the top of Empress Mountain from the west.

Both of these routes can be accessed from the Galloping Goose Trail.

The Sooke River's unique potholes and smooth, deep pools were caused by glacial action 15,000 years ago. As the melting ice sheets passed by they scoured the soft sandstone and deposited large boulders, which wedged in the river. Strong, surging currents buffeted and twirled the rocks between canyon walls and on the river bottom carving the geological formations we see today. The Sooke River, southern Vancouver Island's second largest and an important spawning grounds for chinook and coho, is a great place to view the annual fall salmon run.

~ ~ ~

In 1849, Captain Walter Colquhoun Grant arrived in Victoria from Scotland, as official surveyor for the Hudson's Bay company. He settled in Sooke where he planted about a dozen seeds of Scottish broom which has since spread throughout many parts of Vancouver Island. Though beautiful, when its yellow blooms cover the roads and hillsides in May and June, the plant is too successful and chokes out native species. Here, broom has no enemies and flourishes in its adopted environment.

~ ~ ~

The Harrison Trail is named for the late Claude Harrison, a former Victoria mayor, who, along with the Alpine Club, lobbied for the creation of Sooke Mountain Provincial Park. Three lakes: Sheilds Lake (often misspelled) was called Smokehouse Lake by hunters who once smoked venison nearby, Grass (Grassie) Lake, named for its shoreline reeds, and Crabapple Lake, for the trees around its circumference, were watering stops for pack animals during the Leechtown gold rush in 1864.

**Hike Descriptions:**

If you enjoy strenuous hiking on wilderness routes, this is the place for you. Expect a maze of old roads, indistinct side paths and game trails throughout this remote area. Most routes are poorly marked and not maintained. Some cross open rocky hillsides, others peter out and you may have to bushwhack. It is best to travel with someone familiar with the region. Contact local hiking clubs.

**Harbour View Road** is a rough, mostly uphill "route" with numerous washouts and loose rocks. Part way up the steady ascent along Harbour View Road are several spur roads on the right. The old road in to Mount Manuel Quimper is on the right side about 2 km from the gate. The

Quimper summit (540 m) is accessed via rough, obscure routes that travel mostly uphill. Closer to the top, the trail narrows and there are washouts and loose rocks. About 8 km in, and just outside the park's northern boundary, the old road divides. Turn left and a steep climb up the old road base will take you to Sheilds Lake. Grass (Grassie) Lake lies further to the west. Keep straight on and you will end up at Crabapple Lake. Today they are good lakes to fish and popular camping spots. Continuing beyond Crabapple Lake, if you know the territory, you can journey all the way to the top of Empress Mountain (673 m). The summit views are unmatched.

**Camp Thunderbird**, a YM-YWCA camp has developed good bush trails around their facility. From Sooke Road, cut right (north) onto Glinz Lake Road (just west of Gillespie Road) and continue to the camp. The sign-posted trails here are open to the public from mid-October to mid-April but you must obtain permission before hiking there. Contact: victoriay.com for details.

**Camp Barnard**, a Scouts Canada campground, offers a steep, rocky trail up to a hilltop viewpoint on Bluff Mountain (535 m) and a delightful loop trail around Young Lake (5.7 ha). In Sooke, turn right from Sooke Road onto Otter Point Road and continue for about 5 km to Young Lake Road. Turn right and follow the signposts to the camp. Public access information is available at: victoria.cascadia.scouts.ca.

**Take your camera**
Remember to take your camera. Walking or hiking on local trails is a perfect opportunity to take photos of your family, friends, scenery and wildlife and provides a memory of a great day in the outdoors.

## Bald Eagles, Ospreys and Turkey Vultures

Bald Eagles feed on both carrion and fish. A Bald Eagle will sit for hours in a tall tree or snag, looking out over the water for fish swimming on the surface. When one is spotted it launches from its perch, flies and glides toward the intended meal, which it deftly snatches out of the water with outstretched talons. As it flies back to perch, marauding gulls will often try to make the eagle drop its prey.

Ospreys live entirely on fish and hunt persistently over lakes and estuaries, alternately flying and soaring for hours. When a prospective meal is seen, they hover with rapid wing beats before diving headfirst into the water becoming completely immersed. Moments later they burst to the surface and into the air with struggling wing beats. At the first opportunity, the osprey will shake the water from its feathers, with a burst of water droplets, much like a dog shaking water from its coat.

Turkey Vultures live off carrion, which they locate by smell and eat at its source. You will normally see vultures only in flight and seldom see them gorging on their "find".

Photo: George Broome

# 26. West Coast Road:
# Sooke to Port Renfrew

Photo: Aldyth Hunter

## 26. West Coast Road: Sooke to Port Renfrew

**Highlights:** Highway #14 (West Coast Road) stretches almost 73 km from Sooke to Port Renfrew and is the gateway to the Juan de Fuca Trail. The seascapes enroute are unforgettable and several wild west coast beaches can be accessed via scenic rainforest trails. There are opportunities for wildlife viewing, nature appreciation and birdwatching.

**Difficulty/Distance:** easy to strenuous/varies

**Cautions:** Use precautions against wood ticks. Avoid low bushes and tall grasses. These parasites are most problematic between March and June.

Area rainforests are prime habitat for black bear and cougar. Be alert when hiking, particularly when travelling with small children.

Be prepared for torrential rains, dense sea fog and severe, blustery winds, which may occur at any time of the year and with little warning. West coast weather is capricious, at best.

When beach hiking, beware of unexpected rogue waves. Check the tide tables carefully to avoid becoming marooned by high water. Tidal knowledge is crucial along many trails as headlands may be impassable at high tide. Storms and steady winds may increase the heights of predicted high water.

You may encounter logging trucks and other industrial traffic along the West Coast Road and area logging roads. Always yield the right-of-way and drive defensively. Use your headlights. Improvements and widening of the road from Port Renfrew to Cowichan Lake has made this route a viable alternate access to the region.

**Access:** From Victoria, take Highway #14 (West Coast Road) to Sooke. Using the intersection of the West Coast Road and Otter Point Road in Sooke as the Km-0 mark, continue west and enjoy. (See map on page 140.)

Sooke to Port Renfrew (All distances approximate.)

| Km 0 | West Coast Road (Highway #14)/Otter Point Road intersection in Sooke (traffic lights) |
|---|---|
| Km 1.7 | Whiffin Spit Road (access to Whiffin Spit hiking) |
| Km 21.7 | French Beach (trail to beach) |
| Km 28.7 | Sandcut Creek Trail (trail to beach) |
| Km 32.5 | Jordan River bridge |
| Km 35.3 | China Beach campground (trail to beach) |

| | |
|---|---|
| Km 36.7 | China Beach day-use area (trail to beach/ Juan de Fuca Trail access #1) |
| Km 56.8 | Sombrio Beach (trail to beach/ Juan de Fuca Trail access #2) |
| Km 66.4 | Parkinson Creek access road (trail to beach/ Juan de Fuca Trail access #3) |
| Km 72.4 | Port Renfrew Recreation Centre/Deering Road junction (right turn for Cowichan Lake, Fairy and Lizard lakes) |
| Km 74.3 | Cerantes Road (keep left for Botanical Beach/ Juan de Fuca Trail access #4) |

Starting at the junction of the West Coast Road and Otter Point Road in Sooke, continue west. Whiffin Spit Road (Km 1.7) leads to great hiking at Whiffin Spit Park. (See page 120.) At Km 10.4 you will see the wide expanse of Gordon's Beach. Look for the Sheringham Point lighthouse in the distance. The Sheringham Point Lighthouse Preservation Society is working towards the creation of a community park at the site.

**Access to French Beach (Km 21.7):** French Beach Provincial Park (59 ha) is a serviced, 69-site campground along West Coast Road. From Victoria, allow 45 minutes driving time. The picnic/day-use area and toilets are wheelchair accessible.

**Hike Description:**

**French Beach Trail** (easy/100 m, one way): From the parking lot, a short (5 to 10 minutes), easy trail leads to French Beach. The shoreline view from the beautiful pebble and sand beach takes in Juan de Fuca Strait and the Olympic Mountains. The surf on this somewhat exposed shoreline can be impressive. Explore the 1.6 km beach from the north end, near the group camping area, all the way south, to where a trail curves inland at Goudie Creek.

Other trails wind through the park's second-growth forest (Douglas-fir, western red cedar, western hemlock and Sitka spruce) and salt marsh. One trail, close to the parking lot, parallels Frenchome Creek and connects the beach with the West Coast Road.

**Worth Noting:**

- Water is available at the French Beach campground.
- No beach fires are allowed.

■ French Beach is named for James George French, who settled in this area around 1890, and was a pioneer conservationist.

**Access to Sandcut Creek Trail (Km 28.7):** The trailhead is not sign-posted along the West Coast Road but this trail is worth exploring. Watch for a roadside pulloff, on the left. From Victoria, allow 1 hour driving time.

**Hike Description:**

**Sandcut Creek Trail** (easy/250 m, one way): A pretty rain forest trail (15 minutes down; 20 minutes up) with a moderately steep descent leads from the West Coast Road to the beach. In wet weather the trail can be very muddy and the boardwalks slippery. Salal thickets, huckleberries, Oregon grape and a variety of ferns line the route. Look for large stumps with notches in them, dating back to the hand-logging era. These cuts are where early loggers inserted springboards to assist in tree falling.

Near the sea the trail levels off, negotiates some boardwalks and crosses McManus Creek. After a small hill the path emerges on a long sand and pebble beach. A shoreline highlight is where Sandcut Creek splits into two waterfalls near tidewater. To the east you will spot Point No Point. A low tide beach walk from Sandcut Creek to Jordan River is about 3 km, one way. Desolation Creek, at the halfway point, must be forded and may be impassable when in flood. The beach trail ends at the Western Forest Products parking lot, just east of the Jordan River bridge.

Western Forest Products (the logging company that maintains the Sandcut Creek Trail) provides a recreation site, near the mouth of the Jordan River, with ample parking, a picnic site, toilets, fire pits and picnic tables. This location is often lined with campers and RVs. The Jordan River bridge is at Km 32.5.

**Access to China Beach (Km 35.3/Km 36.7):** The entrance to the 78-site China Beach campground is on the left at Km 35.3. A trail from the campground descends to Second Beach. Continue just over a kilometre west to reach the China Beach day-use area, the first (southern) of four access points for the Juan de Fuca Trail. Turn left at Km 36.7 to the lower parking area. A trail begins here and goes down to China Beach. (The upper parking lot is for Juan de Fuca Trail users.) From Victoria to China Beach, allow 1.5 hours driving time.

**Hike Descriptions:**

**China Beach Trails** (moderate/1 km, one way): From the China Beach campground a steep, 1 km trail, with a series of seemingly never-ending stairs, leads to the cobble shoreline at Second Beach.

There are benches en route to the beach. From the China Beach day-use area trailhead (in the lower parking area) a 1 km gravel trail plunges through the forest to sandy China Beach. A viewing platform offers vistas of Juan de Fuca Strait and the beach. Hike west to a waterfall or east along the shoreline between Second and China beaches. There are very large Sitka spruce (some hundreds of years old and 60 m tall) in this area. Each trail takes about 15-20 minutes to hike, one way. Allow extra time for the climb back up.

**China Beach to Mystic Beach** (moderate to strenuous/2.5 km, one way): From the upper parking lot at the China Beach day-use area, follow the signposted trail west to Mystic Beach. This is the first (or last) campsite on the Juan de Fuca Trail and the beach is very busy on weekends. The trail rises and falls a fair bit and some hills are steep. Watch for muddy patches and large roots. The Pete Wolf Creek suspension bridge is a highlight. In the final stretch to the beach the trail narrows and turns steep. At one point you must traverse a large, fallen log, out of which rough, high steps have been hewn. Be extremely careful here. Once at tidewater, turn east to a waterfall that pours down a high sandstone bluff, behind the cobble and sand beach. Remember to dress warmly; Mystic Beach can be windy.

**Worth Noting:**

- Common birds to watch for here and in other coastal regions are Steller's Jays, grouse, Varied Thrushes, woodpeckers, warblers, ravens, Belted Kingfishers, Rufous Hummingbirds, sparrows, Winter Wrens and many more.
- Water is available at the China Beach campground.
- Beach fires are not permitted.

**Access to Sombrio Beach (Km 56.8):** A few kilometres west of the Loss Creek bridge watch for the Sombrio Beach trailhead turnoff, on the left at Km 56.8. It's about 2.2 km down a rough, steep access road to the parking area and trailhead. You may encounter loose gravel at the switchbacks. This second access point to the Juan de Fuca Trail is a popular destination for day hikers. From Victoria, allow 2 hours driving time.

**Hike Description:**

**Sombrio Beach Trail** (easy/250 km, one way): From the parking lot a gravel trail, with a few steep parts, meanders through a second-growth forest. A little before the beach there is a signposted junction. The right fork (marked Kuitshe Creek) leads west along the Juan de Fuca Trail to a suspension bridge over Sombrio River and the West Sombrio Beach campsite. The beach on this side of the river is strewn with cobblestones and boulders which makes walking difficult.

Keep left at the junction and continue through a small stand of old-growth trees to the beach and the East Sombrio campsites. You can explore the shoreline southeast for about 1 km. The beach is sandy and rocky and has some tidal shelves. At its south end an orange marker ball hanging in the trees indicates the beach access to the Juan de Fuca Trail. From here you can extend your hike to Sombrio Point or Loss Creek, but start early in the day. Expect to do lots of tiring up-and-down climbing beyond East Sombrio Beach, on a rough route with muddy and overgrown sections.

**Access to Parkinson Creek trailhead (Km 66.4):** From the Sombrio cutoff, continue west on the West Coast Road towards Port Renfrew. The Parkinson Creek access road is on the left at Km 66.4. This rough, narrow secondary road twists and turns for 3.8 km to the parking area. The Parkinson Creek trailhead is the third access point for the Juan de Fuca Trail. On the way in there are numerous spur roads; generally keep right when in doubt. From Victoria, allow 2 hours, 20 minutes driving time.

**Hike Description:**

**Parkinson Creek Trail:** From the parking area, a moderately difficult trail follows an old logging road and snakes through slash and clearcuts near Parkinson Creek to the beach access, a little over 1 km away. Low tide reveals exposed tide pools on the beach's rocky shelf.

At the bottom of a long grade the West Coast Road curves left to meet Deering Road (Km 72.4) near the Port Renfrew Recreation Centre. Stop in for trail and tourist information.

**Access to Botanical Beach (Km 74.3):** From the West Coast Road/Deering Road junction in Port Renfrew continue straight ahead on West Coast Road to Cerantes Road, near the government wharf. Turn left onto Cerantes Road and head west for 3 km to the parking lot and trailhead. Botanical Beach is the fourth (northern) access to the Juan de Fuca Trail. From Victoria, allow about 2.5 hours driving time.

**Hike Descriptions:**

**Mill Bay Trail** (moderate/1 km, one way) Part way in to the Botanical Beach parking lot you will pass the signpost (on the right) for the Mill Bay Trail. The somewhat steep trail drops quickly at first and then gradually levels out as it nears sea level at Mill Bay. This partially protected cove on Port San Juan features a shell and pebble shoreline. Low tide is the best time to investigate the cave at one end of the beach.

**Botanical Beach Loop** (moderate/3 km loop): From the parking area it is possible to loop around the Botanical Beach area in either direction. The trail to the right leads 0.5 km to Botany Bay and the one on the left follows an old logging road 1 km to Botanical Beach. Seaward, a high, sandstone headland separates these shorelines, but a 1.5 km inland trail links them. When tides are low enough you can follow the shelf right around the headland. At higher tides use the headland bypass route. Beach access points are marked by orange balls hanging in trees. Boardwalks cross muddier sections of the trail. At Botanical Beach's east end the Juan de Fuca Trail continues east along the coast.

The big feature at Botanical Beach is the relative ease with which you can see a profusion of intertidal marine life exposed on the sandstone shelf. Within the sea-carved tidal pools (one called the Devil's Billiard Table) you may encounter sea star, sea anemones, barnacles, mussels, sea cucumber, plant life and small fish. Some deeper pools may even harbour a small octopus. Never touch, disturb or remove any tidepool life.

---

Botanical Beach's uniqueness, with tidal pools filled with a variety of marine life, is of particular interest to marine biologists and other naturalists. Dr. Josephine Tilden chose it as the site of the University of Minnesota's marine station in 1900. Access at that time was by steamship from Victoria to Port Renfrew, then on foot along a muddy track. This difficult access was a contributing factor in the station's closure in 1907.

---

**Worth Noting:**

- Very low (1.2 m and less) or minus tides are most desirable for tidepool viewing. Be sure to have precise tidal information prior to your hike. Remember to add one hour for Daylight Saving Time.

- Periodically and unpredictably an unusually large wave (rogue wave) or a series of larger waves will hit the beach. These dangerous waves can sweep unsuspecting visitors into the water. Never allow children to play near the surf. Be extra careful when crossing surge channels.

- The shoreline and sandstone shelf is rocky and slippery. Wear proper footwear.

- No camping or fires are permitted at Botanical Beach. The nearest walk-in campsites are located 6 km to the east, along the Juan de Fuca Trail.

In the San Juan River Valley, east of Port Renfrew, are two easy-to-get-to hiking destinations.

**Access to Fairy Lake:** From the Port Renfrew Recreation Centre, take Deering Road, cross the bridge over the San Juan River's south arm and continue north to a second bridge (over the river's north arm) and T-junction. (Gordon Main is to the left.) Turn right onto Harris Creek Main and follow the signs for Cowichan Lake. Approximately 2 km east of the T-junction, opposite a small rock quarry, watch for the trailhead, on the right.

## Hike Description:

**Fairy Lake Nature Trail:** (moderate/1 km, one way): The trail runs from the mainline through second-growth timber to the BC Forest Service Fairy Lake campsite. About 100 m before the campsite is Stoney Creek, which flows into Fairy Lake. In the summer months it is easy to cross; in the wet season the stream may be impassable, forcing hikers to backtrack. Turn right onto the old logging road you crossed on the way in for an alternate route out.

**Access to Lizard Lake:** From Port Renfrew take Deering Road to the Gordon Main/Harris Creek Main T-junction. Turn right onto Harris Creek Main and continue 12.5 km to the Lens Creek Main junction. Keep left on Harris Creek Main (following the Cowichan Lake signs) and travel another 1.5 km to the entrance for the BC Forest Service Lizard Lake campsite. Just beyond the recreation site look for an old logging road (blocked) on the right. Park well off the road. The trail begins to your left and heads east.

## Hike Description:

**Lizard Lake Nature Trail:** (moderate/1.5 loop) The Lizard Lake Trail is rough and zigzags around Lizard Lake, but at some distance from it, so the trail can be quite dark. There are plenty of blowdowns in the surrounding forest. The trail skirts the lake's west end campsite to emerge onto Harris Creek Main once again. Allow 35 minutes to complete the loop.

## Worth Noting:

- Vancouver Island's wilderness beaches and trails offer excellent opportunities to observe marine life. Spring and fall brings the migrating Grey whales. Scan the waves for killer whales, sea lions, seals and otters. Ospreys, Bald Eagles, gulls, cormorants and a variety of seabirds are plentiful.
- Wear good footwear. Please keep to designated trails.
- Tide tables are posted at some trailheads.
- Contact BC Parks for information on day-use parking fees, campground fees and camping reservations for French Beach and China Beach. (See page 167.)

**For The Juan de Fuca Marine Trail:** For a more detailed description of the 47-km Juan de Fuca Marine Trail, see page 140.

**For The West Coast Trail**, see page145.

**San Juan River Valley Trails:** There are other rugged San Juan River Valley trails to explore near Port Renfrew. Varying in length from 0.5 to 6 km, they lead to river sandbars, a waterfall, a plank road, the site of a former railway logging camp, along an old railway grade and to large trees. The trailhead for Port Renfrew's most famous tree, the Red Creek Fir, is the hardest to reach since the deteriorating 12 km access road is rough and often impassable. Some of the area's trails are difficult to locate, receive scant maintenance and are often seasonally flooded. Contact: portrenfrew.com for directions, maps, updates and further information.

Until 1996, the Red Creek Fir was Canada's tallest known Douglas-fir with the following dimensions: circumference at chest height, 12.6 m; diameter 4 m; height to its twice-broken top, 74 m. Its age is estimated to be between 850 and 1,000 years.

The record as the tallest known Douglas-fir in Canada has now passed to a towering giant in the Coquitlam River watershed, on the BC mainland. The 94.3 m-high newcomer is taller, but slimmer, a mere 8 m in circumference. It's younger, too, at around 800 years. In its prime, the Red Creek Fir probably outstripped both the Coquitlam tree and the giant Sitka spruce in the Carmanah Valley. Newer measurements have confirmed that the Red Creek Fir is the world's "largest" known Douglas-fir, containing 349 cubic metres of wood – a greater board measure of timber than the mainland upstart.

*Juan de Fuca Trail near Soule Creek*

Photo: Joyce Folbigg

# R27. Juan de Fuca Trail

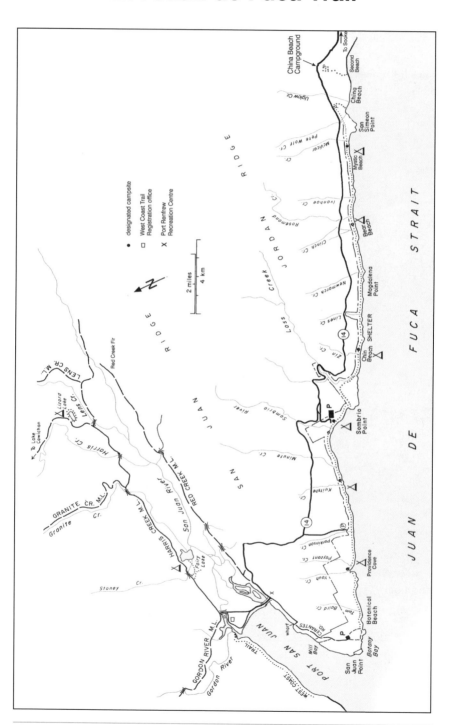

# R27. Juan de Fuca Trail

**Highlights:** The Juan de Fuca Marine Trail, within Juan de Fuca Provincial Park (1528 ha), stretches 47 km along Vancouver Island's wild west coast. Extending from China Beach to Botanical Beach, near Port Renfrew, the trail features wilderness hiking and camping, breathtaking seascapes and excellent opportunities for wildlife viewing, nature appreciation and birdwatching. The trail leads to waterfalls, old growth rainforests of western red cedar, hemlock and Sitka spruce, ravines, estuaries, surf-lashed beaches, tidepools, sea stacks and rocky headlands. Your options are varied. From any of the four designated trailheads, take a day hike to a nearby beach or head off on a more challenging overnight or multi-day jaunt. (See the West Coast Road section on page 130 for details on day hikes.)

**Difficulty/Distance:** moderate to strenuous/47 km, one way

**Cautions:** The more remote parts of the Juan de Fuca Trail are best suited for experienced hikers, familiar with multi-day treks in a wilderness setting. Allow at least 4 to 5 days for the complete hike.

Be prepared. Before starting your hike, check for a map and the latest trail information at BC Parks website: env.gov.bc.ca/bcparks

Leave a detailed trip itinerary with someone reliable at home. Never hike alone and allow ample time for a return journey. BC Parks recommends you leave your pets at home.

Be self-sufficient and carry emergency supplies. Pack out everything you bring in.

Carry your own water on day hikes. Water is available at streams. Always boil, treat or filter water before drinking.

Keep to designated trails and campsites to protect sensitive vegetation. Do not disturb or remove any plants, animals or marine life.

To safely hike many of the trail's beach and sandstone shelf sections requires timing and the proper low tides. Be sure to have precise tidal information prior to your trip. Tide tables are posted at each trailhead. Remember to add one hour for Daylight Saving Time. Storms and steady winds may increase the heights of predicted high water.

Tides may be problematic near Bear Beach's east end; at two spots at Chin Beach and at three separate headlands near Sombrio Point. Recurring slope failure at West Sombrio Bluff has blocked the headland bypass trail there.

Hikers must follow the 0.6-km beach route and time their passage carefully with favourable lower tides.

Some headlands (not all) may be skirted via bypass trails. Beach access points are marked by orange balls hanging in shoreline trees. When hiking on beaches, around headlands, on the tidal shelf and near surge channels beware of unexpected, unusually large rogue waves or a series of larger waves. Hikers have been swept off the rocks. Keep children safely away from the surf.

Trails are usually muddy, root-prone and regularly climb up and down steep terrain in the numerous creek valleys. There are switchbacks and dense brush. Boardwalks and log crossings may be slippery. Use extreme caution along cliff edges, bluffs and open rock faces. The shoreline and sandstone shelf is rocky and slippery. Some beaches consist of rocks and large boulders. Use a staff or trekking pole. Travel slowly and wear proper footwear.

Prepare for torrential rains, dense sea fog and strong, gale force winds, which may occur at any time of the year and with little warning. Creeks and streams flood quickly and some may be impassable following heavy rains.

Area rainforests are prime habitat for black bear and cougar. Be alert when hiking, particularly when traveling with children. If available, use the bear caches at designated campsites or hang your food securely in trees. Cook food away from camp.

Nesting wasps are prevalent along parts of the trail.

Driftwood campfires are permitted but only on beaches and below the high tide line. No fires are allowed at the China Beach day-use area, Botanical Beach or the designated forest campsites at Little Kuitshe or Payzant Creeks. Use a camp stove and set up your tent at the provided camping pads.

You may meet logging trucks and other industrial traffic along the winding West Coast Road. Always yield the right-of-way and drive defensively. Use your headlights. Slow down and yield to oncoming traffic at the one-lane bridges.

**Access:** Four designated trailheads for the Juan de Fuca Marine Trail are located along the West Coast Road (Highway #14). Distances to each, from the junction of the West Coast Road and Otter Point Road in Sooke (Km 0) are: China Beach 36.7 km; Sombrio Beach 56.8 km; Parkinson Creek 66.4 km and Botanical Beach via Cerantes Road 77.5 km.

The Juan de Fuca Trail is open all year. Hikers must self-register at the trailheads. Except in the off-season, fees apply for overnight and multi-day hikes with trailhead parking included. Consult the BC Parks web site and map prior to your hike for current information, cautions and closures. Check also on fees for reservations and overnight stays at the China Beach campground. (See page 167.)

At the trailheads, study the signposted maps carefully to familiarize yourself with the trail and expected conditions. Carry good maps (ideally a topographical map) and be sure to have accurate tide information. Kilometre signposts are situated along the length of the trail. GPS units and cell phones may not work in all parts of the park.

**Hike Descriptions:**

**China Beach to Sombrio Beach** (strenuous/29 km, one way): This stretch of the Juan de Fuca Trail traverses rough terrain and is best hiked over two or even three days, with overnight stops at Bear Beach (Km 9) and Chin Beach (Km 21).

From the China Beach trailhead the trail leads 2.5 km west to Mystic Beach, the trail's first (or last) campsite. This is a popular day hiking destination. From Mystic Beach to Bear Beach the trail keeps to the forest, but there are viewpoints along the cliffs west of Mystic Beach. Expect muddy sections at any time of the year. August is often the driest month. West of Ivanhoe Creek the trail slowly drops to Bear Beach. The shoreline here is covered with slick stones and hard to traverse. Camp on the beach at the designated campsites.

The 12 km section from Bear Beach to Chin Beach is considered the toughest part of the hike and it can be very muddy. Elevation changes are endless since the trail continually rises and falls in every creek valley. The trail stays mainly in the forest until the slow descent to Chin Beach. An emergency cabin is located at the trail's 20.5-m mark if tides cut off the approach to Chin Beach's east side. There are several spots to pitch a tent at Chin Beach and numerous beach access trails.

About 3 km west of Chin Beach is the Loss Creek suspension bridge, a hike highlight. Take some time to savour the view. The trail then curves inland, follows an old logging road and turns back toward the coast to hug the cliffs on the approach to Sombrio Beach. Beach camping is permitted at East Sombrio Beach (Km 27) and on the tent platforms at West Sombrio Beach campsite (Km 29). In between is the cutoff to the Sombrio Beach parking lot and trailhead.

**Sombrio Beach to Parkinson Creek** (strenuous/8 km, one way): From Sombrio Beach the Juan de Fuca Trail heads west to cross the Sombrio River suspension bridge to the West Sombrio Beach campsite (with tent platforms). Due to slope failure near West Sombrio bluff, the bypass trail is severed. The beach route is the only option. Time your passage carefully for low tide. The up and down hiking in the creek valleys continues west of Sombrio Beach, but the hills are less steep. Fording the mouth of Minute Creek is hazardous on a high tide. Hike inland to the suspension bridge to cross this stream. Consider a stopover at the designated inland campsite at Little Kuitshe Creek (Km 33). The trail continues west, through logged forest to the Parkinson Creek trailhead (Km 37).

**Parkinson Creek to Botanical Beach** (moderate/10 km, one way): This final stretch of the Juan de Fuca Trail is a lot easier to hike than the eastern sections but there are still some elevation changes, muddy sections, uneven terrain and roots to contend with. Forest camping is available at Payzant Creek (Km 40) on the provided tent platforms. From here, the trail continues inland to a well-built bridge over Yauh Creek. A side trail leads to picturesque Providence Cove.

If the tides are low enough, hike the last 4 or 5 km via the beach. The inland trail has boardwalks over wet and muddy areas. There are many beach access points. Try to time your arrival at Botanical Beach with low tide. Tides of 1.2 m or lower are ideal for exploring diverse marine life in exposed tidepools on the sandstone shelf. From the east end of Botanical Beach (Km 46) follow an old logging road 1 km to the parking lot and trailhead. Extend your hike by heading west, past a headland, to Botany Bay and then take a second access trail to the trailhead. (See page 135.)

**Worth Noting:**

- Suspension bridges have been installed at the Sombrio River and also at Pete Wolf, Loss and Minute creeks. The views from these spans are outstanding.

- Watch for sea lions, seals, killer whales, other large marine mammals and marine birds off the points of land. Grey whales migrate north along the coast in March and April and return south in the fall.

- The Juan de Fuca Trail does not connect with the West Coast Trail. For information on trailhead bus service contact: trailbus.com.

**Nearby:**
For descriptions of more West Coast Road and Port Renfrew shoreline hikes see page 131.

**West Coast Trail:** The Gordon River trailhead, near Port Renfrew, is the southern terminus of the West Coast Trail. This arduous 75 km trail extends north from Port Renfrew to Pachena Bay, close to Bamfield. The West Coast Trail is recommended for experienced backpackers only, those familiar with multi-day jaunts. You must be fit and well-equipped. A daily quota system limiting hiking starts applies. Contact Parks Canada at: pc.gc.ca for current details on reservation fees, ferry services and overnight use permits. The West Coast Trail is closed during the hazardous off-season.

# R28. Galloping Goose Trail

Photo: Aldyth Hunter

## R28. Galloping Goose Trail

**Highlights:** The CRD's multi-use Galloping Goose Regional Trail stretches 55 km, from downtown Victoria to Sooke and into the mountains of the Sooke River Valley. Hikers, bikers, joggers, horse riders and commuters use the route, which follows an old CNR rail line right-of-way. There are countless opportunities for urban walks and wildlife viewing. The trail runs close to parks, scenic lookouts and beaches. The CRD's 11-page brochure "The Official Guide to the Galloping Goose Regional Trail" is available at crd.bc.ca/parks/brochure. There are large-scale maps and the brochure covers in detail the entire 55 km.

**Difficulty/Distance:** easy to moderate/55 km in length

**Cautions:** The Selkirk Trestle can be slippery following rains.

Proceed with caution at the many street crossings.

**Access:** Designated free parking lots are located at Atkins Road, near the Highway #1 (Trans-Canada) overpass; off Sooke Road at Aldeane Avenue and at Glen Lake Road; off Happy Valley Road at Bilston Creek; off Rocky Point Road at Kangaroo Road and closer to Matheson Lake; at Roche Cove Regional Park (wheelchair accessible toilets). Parking fees apply at the two parking lots along Sooke River Road, one south of Sooke Potholes Provincial Park, the other to the north, at Sooke Potholes Regional Park. You can get on and off the Galloping Goose at many points along its length. The trail is open from sunrise to sunset.

**Hike Description:**

The Galloping Goose begins east of the Johnson Street bridge, where the kilometre markers begin, and then follows the Selkirk Waterway. One of the trail's highlights is the 300-m-long Selkirk Trestle over the Gorge's Selkirk Waters. The trestle, built from hemlock and fir, is five metres wide. The route goes through Cecelia Ravine and alongside a restored part of Cecelia Creek to a light industrial area near Douglas Street.

At the 4-km mark is the Switch Bridge, a 100-m pedestrian overpass over Highway #1 (Trans-Canada) near the Town and Country Shopping Centre. This is the junction with the Lochside Trail, a 29-km multi-use corridor stretching north up the Saanich Peninsula to Swartz Bay. (See page 152.)

The Galloping Goose swings west from the Switch Bridge to parallel Highway #1 (Trans-Canada). There are some up and down sections as you pass through View Royal. At the 10.5-km mark is the Atkins Road parking lot where there are toilets. Nearby Six Mile Road accesses Thetis Lake

Regional Park. The route crosses Millstream Creek on a sturdy bridge near the falls, which are especially striking on cold, bright days in winter.

The trail roughens somewhat as the loose surface (packed dirt) begins. Watch for dips and dives, bumps and the occasional impeding branch, muddy stretch or puddle. Pay attention at the many street crossings as you wind through Colwood and Langford. Though generally flat, the trail does have hilly sections. Possible side trips include Fort Rodd Hill/Fisgard Lighthouse National Historic Site, just over a kilometre down Ocean Boulevard or the many walking trails near Hatley Castle at Royal Roads University. The parking lot at Sooke and Glen Lake roads, close to the Luxton Fairgrounds, is at the 18-km mark.

The Galloping Goose enters Metchosin to pass through pastures, farmlands, rocky outcrops and hills. The trail roughly parallels Happy Valley Road for 7 km to the junction of Kangaroo and Rocky Point roads. A 1.5-km side trip east along Rocky Point Road, then Happy Valley Road to William Head Road will bring you to the historic Metchosin School. It opened in 1871 and is one of Western Canada's first public schools. Lombard Road (near the 26-km mark) leads to Devonian Regional Park, along William Head Road. (See page 103.)

From the second Rocky Point Road parking lot, south of Malloch Road near the 30-km mark, the trail narrows and heads west for 4.5 km through Matheson Lake, then Roche Cove regional parks. Here the route's semi-wilderness nature emerges. (See pages 105 and 107.) The parking lot at Roche Cove's west end has wheelchair-accessible toilets. Use extreme caution at the nearby Gillespie Road crossing owing to a blind curve in the road.

The Galloping Goose runs north to a particularly scenic stretch which skirts numerous rocky headlands and pocket coves along Sooke Basin. You can access this area via Manzer Road, just past Glinz Lake Road. Near Hutchison Cove the route plunges down to Veitch Creek, where the old railway right-of way seems almost to hang out over the water. Take the time to stop near the bridge and savour the view of Veitch Creek. Note: From Veitch Creek to Sooke Potholes Regional Park is around 10 km, one way, about a 3 hour hike.

At Cooper Cove the trail crosses the busy Sooke Road. Next is the CRD's Ayum Creek Reserve (6.2 ha) which protects important salmon habitat near Goodrich Peninsula. NO Dogs are allowed here. Swans frequent these waters. The shoreline at the estuary is a good birdwatching spot. Look for Great Blue Herons, Bald Eagles, Ospreys, shorebirds and other waterfowl. Boxes atop lofty poles provide nesting areas for a variety of birds, including the Purple Martin songbird. You can also reach the reserve by parking off Sooke Road, on the east side of the Ayum Creek bridge, near the 5600 block of Sooke Road. A creekside trail, steep near the bridge, drops to tidewater. The path can be marshy and muddy at the tidal flats. Tread lightly in this environmentally fragile region. Ayum Creek is also known as Stoney Creek.

The Galloping Goose Trail follows the right-of-way of an old Canadian National Railway line. Originally part of the Canadian Northern Pacific Railway, construction of the Victoria to Leechtown section began in 1911. The CNR transported mainly logs and freight. In 1922, the company operated passenger cars between Victoria and Sooke; the service was extended to Youbou, three years later.

The type of coach employed was a clamorous gasoline-powered railbus (Number 15813) known as the "Galloping Goose". These were common throughout Canada. One person handled all the duties of conductor, engineer and baggage handler. In 1931, the CNR abandoned its passenger service. Freight service along a spur line continued sporadically until the late 1970s, then ended. The tracks were removed a few years later.

~ ~ ~

The Leech River and Leechtown were named after Peter John Leech, who arrived with the Royal Engineers in 1858. Leech stayed on, to be part of the Vancouver Island Exploration Expedition in 1864, at which time gold was discovered in the Leechtown area. By 1865, the mining boom was pretty much over, with Victoria merchants and outfitters profiting more than most of the miners. Leechtown soon evaporated into a ghost town.

Eventually the route leaves the lowlands behind, swings north up the Sooke River Valley. The highlights here are the impressive river canyon and potholes. There is a designated parking lot off Sooke River Road (near the 45-km marker, approximately 500 m past Meota Drive) and another at the 48-km marker. The latter provides access to the CRD's Sooke Potholes Regional Park. Please stay on the Galloping Goose Trail between the two parking lots to avoid trespassing on private property. (For more on Sooke Potholes Regional Park, see page 124.)

From the potholes area the trail leads up to the refurbished trestles on Charters and Todd creeks. This is where most trail travelers turn around. You can continue north from Todd Creek on a steady 8-km climb up the Sooke River Valley. This is the most remote part of the Galloping Goose Trail and somewhat narrow and overgrown by trailside trees and bushes. The trail ends a little south of Leechtown, a deserted mining town. Nothing remains today.

**Worth Noting:**

- Consideration between user groups is encouraged, with cyclists giving the right-of-way to hikers and hikers giving way to equestrians. Remember that horses are easily spooked. Safety dictates that all users should keep right, except to pass; courtesy dictates users should alert others when approaching from behind. Contact the CRD for trail updates, information on expected trail etiquette, regional regulations and rules pertaining to the use of electric bicycles.

- Most of the urban sections of the Galloping Goose are paved and many of the unpaved parts, including the section near the Luxton Fairgrounds, are suitable for wheelchair use.

- BC Transit buses (low floor buses with bicycle racks and wheelchair lifts) stop at various points along the trail.

- The Galloping Goose is part of the Trans-Canada Trail, a coast-to-coast multi-use corridor that links Canada's regional trails.

**Nearby:**
The Galloping Goose Trail accesses numerous hiking destinations, parks and beaches. For more information contact CRD Parks. (See page 167.)

*Riding the Goose*

Photo: Aldyth Hunter

# R29. Lochside Trail

Photo: Aldyth Hunter

## R29. Lochside Trail

**Highlights:** The Lochside Trail is a 29-km multi-use corridor that runs from Victoria to Swartz Bay. The trail is popular with hikers, cyclists, joggers and horse riders. The route follows old rail lines and traverses wetlands, rural working agricultural land and urban areas. It is a mix of pavement through residential areas and gravel or dirt surface through farmlands, horse paddocks and fields. The CRD's eight-page brochure "The Official Guide to the Lochside Regional Trail" is available at: crd.bc.ca/parks/brochure. There are large-scale maps and the brochure covers in detail the entire 29 km.

**Difficulty/Distance:** easy, level, some paved/29 km in length

**Cautions:** The trestles can be very slippery on cold days.

In hot weather, carry enough water.

Parts of the trail share or cross public roads. Be alert and watch for traffic.

Farm equipment has the right-of-way.

Rural sections of the trail may be muddy and slippery following heavy rains.

**Access:** The starting point for the Lochside Regional Trail (CRD) is known as the Switch Bridge, a 100-m pedestrian overpass over Highway #1 (Trans-Canada) near the Town and Country Shopping Centre. This start is located at the 4-km mark of the Galloping Goose Regional Trail. Nearby parking is available at the Saanich Municipal Hall and along Saanich Road, north of Lodge Avenue. The trail is open from sunrise to sunset.

**Hike Description:**

From the Switch Bridge the Lochside Trail runs northeast under Blanshard Street and Vernon Avenue and passes the southern fringe of the Swan Lake Christmas Hill Nature Sanctuary. The trail crosses the 30-m Brett and the 140-m Swan Lake Trestle to emerge at Quadra Street. Use caution when crossing here and at the traffic lights at McKenzie Avenue. Continue north on Borden Street and follow the signs to Lochside Drive. At its end there is a parking area close to where the trail turns to gravel. Nearby is the signposted junction with the Blenkinsop Greenway, a trail corridor that links the Lochside Trail with Mount Douglas Park and the Gordon Head area.

Next are the farmlands of the Blenkinsop Valley and a section of trail very familiar to horse riders. Pass with care. A highlight in this area is the 288-m Blenkinsop Trestle spanning Blenkinsop Lake. Stop on the bridge and have your picture taken with Roy. He is always on the bridge. Bird blinds at Blenkinsop Lake Park assist visitors in spotting furtive lakeside wildlife. Just north of the lake you can detour along Lohbrunner Road to Blenkinsop Road and follow the Mercer Trail into Mount Douglas Park, or you can cut west at Donwood Park, a gateway to numerous urban trails in the Broadmead area.

Around the 6-km mark the trail crosses Royal Oak Drive. Opposite McMinn Park, Grant Park features a challenging trail that climbs to the top of Cordova Bay Ridge. Take a break at the Doris Page rest area, where there is a picnic shelter and a great ocean viewpoint looking out on James Island and the San Juan Islands. Doris Page Park provides a link to the Cordova Bay beach. Further north, detour west along Doumac Place to a lushly wooded ravine at Doumac Park.

The trail parallels Cordova Bay Road then picks up Lochside again at Lochside Park, near the 10-km mark. There are seasonal toilets and ample parking here. Expect to encounter horse riders from Lochside Park north to the Island View Road area. A side trip to Elk/Beaver Lake Park is possible via Cordova Bay and Sayward roads.

The Lochside Trail crosses the Saanich/Central Saanich border close to Dooley Road and enters Martindale Valley. This open stretch extends for several kilometres so, in hot weather, carry enough water. At Island View Road you can side trip to Island View Beach, 3 km to the east. (See Nearby.) The trail continues north to pass Heritage Acres, the agricultural and industrial museum operated by the Saanich Historical Artifacts Society. The route then runs through Tsawout First Nations land and parallels Pat Bay Highway (#17).

Just over the 16-km mark you will reach Mount Newton Cross Road. Zigzag right then left onto Lochside Drive. The seascapes of Cordova Channel dominate the backdrop. At North Saanich's Cy Hampton Park, near Bazan Bay, there are toilets and parking. Sidney's Tulista Park, near Washington State's Anacortes ferry terminal, also has parking and toilets, and features a promenade with beach access that is wheelchair accessible. From Sidney the trail continues north alongside Pat Bay Highway and swings inland to Tsehum (Shoal) Harbour. Consider a side trip to Horth Hill. (For a description of Horth Hill trails, see page 28.) The 29-km mark is the northern end of the Lochside Trail, the Swartz Bay ferry terminal.

**Worth Noting:**

- Interpretive signposts are located at numerous points along the route.

- Rare and uncommon breeding species of birds to look for near Blenkinsop Lake include Pied-billed Grebes, Green Herons and Wood Ducks. Wintering waterfowl species include Eurasian Widgeons and Ring-necked Ducks. Watch for eagles, Cooper's Hawks, Peregrine Falcons, swallows and Purple Martins.

- The Martindale Flats are an excellent destination to observe wintering freshwater ducks, raptors and Eurasian Skylarks (an introduced species once common on the Saanich Peninsula, but now increasingly rare.)

- BC Transit buses (low floor buses with bike racks and wheelchair lifts) stop at various points along the Lochside Trail.

- Contact CRD Parks for trail updates, regional regulations and information on the use of electric bicycles. (See page 167.)

**Nearby:**
**Island View Beach (42 ha):** From Victoria, take Highway #17 (Pat Bay) and turn right at the traffic lights onto Island View Road. Next, swing left on Homathko Drive to the parking lot and beach. From Victoria, allow 30 minutes driving time. The park is open sunrise to sunset. This CRD regional park, on the Saanich Peninsula's east side, features one of Victoria's closest sandy beaches. The park offers beach and dune hiking and the great seascapes of Haro Strait, the San Juan Islands and Sidney Spit. Spring and fall are excellent times to observe migrating shorebirds.

Do not trespass on the Tsawout Indian Reserve. When you reach the reserve's southern boundary, return on the inland dune trail. On a minus low tide, a 10-km-one-way beach hike is possible from Island View Beach south to Mount Douglas Park with minimal rock scrambling. En route note the erosion of the Cowichan Head cliffs.

The Lochside Trail accesses numerous hiking destinations, parks and beaches. For more information contact CRD Parks.

The first 2.3 km of The Lochside Trail follows what was known as the Saanich Spur, part of a CNR line abandoned in 1990. Borden Mercantile was the last freight customer. Canadian Northern Pacific Railway built the original rail line in 1917, offering passenger and freight service from Victoria to Pat Bay. The CNR took over operations in the 1920s. When the line was in active use, rail traffic was "switched" between tracks, hence the name "Switch Bridge" at the trailhead. The northern tip of the Lochside Trail follows the old Victoria and Sidney Railway bed.

Photo: Aldyth Hunter

*Meet Roy on the Blenkinsop Trestle*

# Campgrounds

These locations provide you with the opportunity to camp and then hike in the same area.

**Road Accessible Campsites:**

# 8  Goldstream

#25  Sooke Potholes

#26  French Beach

#26  China Beach

#26  Fairy Lake

#26  Lizard Lake

#R29  Lochside Trail,  McDonald Campground

**Walk In Campsites**

#1  Portland Island

#2  Sidney Spit

#R27  Juan de Fuca Marine Trail

# Accessible Areas

**Accessibility** allows a person with limited mobility or a disability to use an area and facilities with minimum assistance.

The following hikes have accessible areas.

**#6 Mount Work.**
The north side of Durrance Lake is accessible.

**#8 Goldstream Park**
The Visitor Centre and several short trails from the day-use parking area are accessible.

**#9 Francis/King Elsie King Interpretive Trail**
The Elsie King Trail is wide enough for wheelchairs or scooters to travel side by side. Most of the trail surface is hard-packed gravel, or boardwalk. The Nature Centre and toilets are also accessible.

**#10 Elk/Beaver Lake**
- **Beaver Beach:** This beach has an accessible parking area, paved trails and accessible toilets.
- **Brookleigh Boat Launch:** The boat launch provides easy and safe access to boats. The toilet facility is also accessible.
- **Elk Lake Fishing Float:** The parking area is reserved for disabled only and toilet facility is accessible.
- **Hamsterly Beach:** The children's playground has accessible equipment. A drinking fountain, toilets and picnic tables are also accessible.
- **10K Trail:** The trail loops around the two lakes and is mostly flat and level. There are some narrow and uneven parts on the east side of Elk Lake, along the Pat Bay Highway.

**#11 Rithet's Bog**
Some assistance will be required on uneven ground. No toilet facilities.

**#12 Mount Douglas**
The main parking lot has a children's playground and picnic area and accessible toilets.

**#13 University of Victoria**
The alumni chip trail is mostly accessible, with some parts requiring assistance. Parking Lot 6, near the Interfaith Chapel and the gardens are accessible.

## #15 Victoria Waterfront
The trail is level and wide enough for wheelchairs or scooters. Toilets are available.

## #16 Swan Lake
The trail to the wooden dock overlooking the lake is accessible.
- **Beckwith Park:** The trail around the park and the toilet facilities are accessible.

## #17 Colquitz River
Most of the trail from Tillicum Mall north to Hyacinth Park is accessible.

## #19 Mill Hill
The trails are not accessible but the picnic area and toilets are.

## #21 Metchosin Shoreline
At Witty's Lagoon, the Nature Centre, picnic area and toilets are accessible. Devonian Park parking lot, picnic area and toilets are accessible.

## #22 Western Metchosin
The Roche Cove toilets are accessible.

## #23 East Sooke -Aylard Farm Picnic Area
The accessible trail connects the parking lot with the picnic shelter and toilet facilities. A steeper trail to the beach could be accessed with assistance.

## #26 West Coast Road -French Beach
The picnic/day-use area and toilets are accessible.

## #R28 Galloping Goose and #R29 Lochside Regional Trail
These connected regional trails are mainly wide and level, with pavement or hard-packed gravel.

## #R29 Lochside Regional Trail -Island View Beach
A group picnic shelter and toilet facilities are accessible.

# Nature Walks

In the Victoria area, almost anywhere you walk or hike in the Spring, will have at least a few native flowers and plants in bloom. The mild climate in the Victoria region allows plant discovery walks all year round. While the spring and summer are the most flamboyant, with showy displays of wildflowers, the fall and winter provide ample opportunity to observe other plants such as fungi, mosses and lichens. This area also has many evergreen trees and shrubs, giving the landscape its green hue year-round. The Victoria Natural History Society (vicnhs.bc.ca) provides walks to many locations. Why not join and take your walks with them?

The Capital Regional District and Saanich also provide spring flower walks to the best locations. Watch the newspapers and look at their web sites. New or used flower and plant guides can be purchased which will add to your enjoyment. Keep on the trails to protect the fragile ecosystems and do not pick the flowers. Often this will kill the plants. Wildflowers do not transplant well so leave these wonderful displays for future generations. Natural areas provide habitat and food for all kinds of creatures, including amphibians, reptiles, insects, small mammals, and birds, many of which nest on the ground. Help protect these creatures by watching where you walk and keeping your dogs under control.

Some of the more spectacular sites are listed below.

## Spring and Summer Flower Walks

**Bear Hill** - There are many wildflowers to see including the delicate Sierra sanicle.

**Beacon Hill Park** - Enjoy the fields of camas and occasionally the yellow paintbrush.

**Finnerty Gardens** - This University of Victoria landmark is known for its spectacular rhododendron and flower garden.

**Francis/King Park** - This 100-year-old forest has some rare plants.

**Gore and Oak Haven Park** - These parks explode with carpets of colourful spring flowers in a Garry oak meadow.

**Gowlland Tod** - Among this area's rare plants are the phantom orchid and some rare mosses.

**Horth Hill** - The rare phantom orchid is sometimes found here along with many other wildflowers.

**Island View Beach** - The beach's fragile sand dune area is habitat to some rare and beautiful plant species.

**Lone Tree Hill** - Among the countless wildflowers here you might spot the albino shooting star.

**Mill Hill** - Look for the pink fairy slipper and as many as 40 species of wildflowers.

**Mount Wells** - This region features many, many varieties of wildflowers. Bring your wildflower field guide.

**Witty's Lagoon** - Look for Fool's onion, harvest brodiaea and Howell's triteleia.

## Fall and Winter Walks

**East Sooke Park** - The headland at Beechey Head is the prime spot to see the annual Turkey Vulture migration or "Hawk Watch" in the fall.

**Goldstream Park** - This park is a popular destination to observe the November salmon runs and for December eagle watching.

**Royal Roads** - Look for mushrooms and fungi in the damp, shady forests.

**Sooke Potholes** - Salmon spawn in the Sooke River in the fall.

**Thetis Lake, Six Mile Road/Millstream Creek** - Enjoy the impressive waterfall and watch for mosses and lichens.

**Witty's Lagoon** - Sitting Lady Falls are especially striking after heavy rains.

**Whiffin Spit** - The spit is an excellent winter birdwatching destination.

*Victoria Natural History Society*

# Birdwatching

When hiking Vancouver Island trails, one can not help noticing the diversity of birds that inhabit our local forests, bays and seashores. Southern Vancouver Island's geography offers a great diversity of habitats from rocky and sandy shoreline and tidal mud flats to deciduous forests, to dense old growth cedar and Douglas-fir stands, and inland rocky hilltops and Garry oak meadows. This diversity attracts an ever changing mix of avifauna and, because our region offers favourable habitats for many bird species, southern Vancouver Island can be a magical place for birdwatching.

September to December are the prime months to birdwatch as summer migrants may linger, vagrants and juveniles wander west, Asian species migrate south, and pelagic species move into Juan de Fuca Strait and Georgia Strait. Late spring offers some great birdwatching opportunities. Some more recognizable rare species that have turned up in our region include: Snowy Owls, Tropical Kingbirds, and Cattle Egrets. Other rare species that seem to make an annual visit include Lazuli Buntings, Rock Sandpipers, Eurasian Wigeons, Brown Pelicans, Short-eared Owls, and Green Herons.

Year round species of interest include: Brandt's Cormorants, Pelagic Cormorants, Marbled Murrelets, Harlequin Ducks, Mute Swans, Glaucous-winged Gulls, Great Blue Herons, Black Oystercatchers, Bald Eagles, Red-tailed Hawks, Anna's Hummingbirds, Sky Larks, California Quail, Bushtits, Bewick's Wrens, as well as many others.

The Victoria Natural History Society (vicnhs.bc.ca) hosts the city's most active birding group and the society regularly schedules field trips to many parks and trails areas. Annual birdwatching hiking excursions include East Sooke Park, Gowlland Tod Park, Mount Tolmie, Island View Beach, Whiffin Spit, and Sidney Island, as well as a host of shorter trail walks to bird viewing locations.

The Capital Regional District's Parks Division (crd.bc.ca/parks) also regularly schedules bird walks on many of our hiking trails. Swan Lake Christmas Hill Nature Sanctuary (swanlake.bc.ca) hosts regular birding walks around the sanctuary every Wednesday and Sunday at 9:00 am.

For more information on birding locations around Greater Victoria and other areas, visit: birding.bc.ca.

## Top Birding Locations

### Blenkinsop Lake
Look for Marsh Wrens, Song Sparrows and Trumpeter Swans (in winter); swallows and Black-headed Grosbeaks (in spring), Bewick's Wrens, Cooper's Hawks and Bushtits.

### East Sooke Park
This is the best place to be in September/October as hundreds of Turkey Vultures kettle here before crossing Juan de Fuca Strait. Many other raptor species, warblers, sparrows, gulls and shorebirds coverage here before departing south. Year round there are Winter Wrens, Chestnut-backed Chickadees and other forest birds.

### Esquimalt Lagoon
This area has a large assortment of gull species, Black Turnstones, Black-bellied Plovers, Mute Swans, Bald Eagles, ducks and Grebes. On both sides of the peninsula watch for Kingfishers, Great Blue Herons, Ospreys and many more. The lagoon is one of the better shorebird stopover points during migration and a great spot for winter birdwatching.

### Goldstream Provincial Park
Observe Red-breasted Sapsuckers, American Dippers, Pileated Woodpeckers and Steller's Jays. Expect to see hundreds of Bald Eagles and thousands of mixed gull species during the fall salmon run.

### Gowlland Tod Provincial Park
You may spot Townsend's Solitaires, Hutton's Vireos, Purple Finch, Solitary Vireos and possibly Golden Eagles among other upland and forest species.

### Martindale Flats/Island View Beach
Watch for Peregrine Falcons, Bald Eagles, Cooper's Hawks, Red-Tailed Hawks and other raptors. You may see Sky Larks, American Pipits and Horned Larks (in migration) and always a mixture of sparrows. In winter the area is home to hundreds of wintering waterfowl including Trumpeter Swans.

### Mount Tolmie
Spring brings Anna's Hummingbirds, warblers and Flycatchers. During migration many rare species have appeared here.

### Rithet's Bog
You might see Virginia Rails, Cooper's Hawks, Song Sparrows, Bushtits and a mixture of duck species.

**Viaduct Flats/Quick's Bottom**
Here you will find an assortment of ducks and shorebirds in migration. Watch for Great Blue Herons, California Quail, many sparrow and warbler species and owls in winter.

**Victoria Waterfront: Ogden Point to Clover Point**
Observe Black Oystercatchers, Surfbirds, Black Turnstones, Glaucous-winged Gulls and other seabirds. This is a great place for discovering rare migrants on top of the shoreline bluff.

**Witty's Lagoon/Tower Point**
This area features a nice mix of habitats for one location. Look for a variety of sparrows, ducks and seabirds and watch for shorebirds and warblers in the spring and fall.

*Kevin Slagboom, Birding in British Columbia*

# Suggested Reading

The books listed below are a random selection of the many titles available to enhance your walking and hiking experience:

**50 Best Dog Walks/Hikes Around Victoria** by Leo Buijs

**Amphibians & Reptiles of British Columbia** by Matsuda, Green & Gregory

**Backroad Map Book  Vol. 2 -Vancouver Island** by Wesley & Russell Mussio

**Backroads Vancouver Island and The Gulf Islands** by Jo Donaldson-Yarmey

**Birder's Guide Vancouver Island: A Walking Guide to Bird Watching Sites** by Keith Taylor

**Birds of Coastal British Columbia** by Nancy Baron & John Acorn

**Birds of Victoria** by Bovey, Campbell & Gates

**Butterflies of British Columbia** by John Acorn

**Coastal Wildflowers of the Pacific Northwest** by Elizabeth L. Horn

**Essential Wilderness Navigator: How to Find Your Way in the Great Outdoors** by David Seidman

**Geology of Southern Vancouver Island** by Chris Yorath

**Hiking Adventures With Children: Southern Vancouver Island and the Olympic Peninsula** by Kari Jones & Sachiko Kiyooka

**Hiking On The Edge: West Coast Trail - Juan de Fuca Trail** by Ian Gill

**Hiking the Gulf Islands** by Charles Kahn

**Hiking the West Coast of Vancouver Island** by Tim Leadem

**Hiking Trails II: South Central Vancouver Island** by Richard K. Blier

**Hiking Trails  III: Northern Vancouver Island including Strathcona Park** by Richard K. Blier

**Hiking Vancouver Island** by Shannon & Lisa Cowan

**Juan de Fuca Marine Trail** by Matthew Payne and Adam Vaselevich

**Nature Walks Around Victoria** by Helen Lansdowne

**Leave No Trace: A Guide to the New Wilderness Etiquette** by Annette McGivney

**Mosses, Lichens & Ferns of Northwest North America** by Vitt, Marsh & Bovey

**Mushrooms of Northwest North America** by Helene Schalkwijk-Barensen

**Native Trees of British Columbia** by Halter & Turner

**Pacific Coast Fern Finder** by Glenn Keaton

**Pacific Coast Bird Finder: A Manual for Identifying 61 Common Birds of the Pacific Coast** by Roger Ledere

**Plants of Coastal British Columbia** by Jim Pojar & Andy Mackinnon

**Plants of The Gulf and San Juan Islands and Southern Vancouver Island** by Collin Varner

**Simple Foods for the Pack: More Than 200 All-Natural, Trail-Tested Recipes** by Claudia Axcell

**Some Common Mosses of British Columbia** by W.B. Schofield

**Trans Canada Trail: The British Columbia Route** by Mussio Ventures

**Vancouver Island Shores** by Linda Colbeck

**Victoria-Nanaimo Nature Walks, The Easy Guide** by John Henigman

**Walk Victoria** by John Crouch

**West Coast Trail: One Step at a Time** by Robert J. Bannon

**Where To See Wildlife on Vancouver Island** by Kim Goldberg

# Information Sources

Check with local municipalities and regional districts, area hiking clubs and outdoor organizations. See the Vancouver Island Trails Information Society (VITIS) website: hikingtrailsbooks.com for addresses.

The following sources provide detailed information and maps:

BC Parks: env.gov.bc.ca/bcparks

Capital Regional District Parks (CRD): crd.bc.ca/parks

Metchosin: district.metchosin.bc.ca

North Saanich: northsaanich.ca

Parks Canada: pc.gc.ca

Port Renfrew: portrenfrew.com

Saanich: gov.saanich.bc.ca

Sooke: sooke.org

Other Contacts:

BC Ferries: bcferries.com (schedules and fares)

BC Transit: bctransit.com (bus information)

Birding In BC: birding.bc.ca

Federation of BC Naturalists: naturalists.bc.ca

Fisheries and Oceans Canada: dfo-mpo.gc.ca (regional tide and current information)

Meteorological Service of Canada: weatheroffice.ec.gc.ca (regional weather information)

Outdoor Club of Victoria: ocv.ca

Vancouver Island Health Authority: viha.ca/mho (health information)

Victoria Natural History Society: vicnhs.bc.ca

# List of Maps

Page

Hiking Areas . . . . . . . . . . . . . . . . . . . . . . . . . . . 9
Portland Island . . . . . . . . . . . . . . . . . . . . . . . . . 20
Sidney Spit . . . . . . . . . . . . . . . . . . . . . . . . . . . . 24
Horth Hill . . . . . . . . . . . . . . . . . . . . . . . . . . . . 28
John Dean . . . . . . . . . . . . . . . . . . . . . . . . . . . . 32
Gowlland Tod . . . . . . . . . . . . . . . . . . . . . . . . . . 36
Mount Work . . . . . . . . . . . . . . . . . . . . . . . . . . . 42
Goldstream/Mount Finlayson . . . . . . . . . . . . . . . . 48
Francis/King . . . . . . . . . . . . . . . . . . . . . . . . . . . 52
Elk/Beaver Lake . . . . . . . . . . . . . . . . . . . . . . . . 56
Mount Douglas . . . . . . . . . . . . . . . . . . . . . . . . . 62
Swan Lake & Christmas Hill . . . . . . . . . . . . . . . . . 78
Colquitz River . . . . . . . . . . . . . . . . . . . . . . . . . 82
Thetis Lake . . . . . . . . . . . . . . . . . . . . . . . . . . . 86
Mill Hill . . . . . . . . . . . . . . . . . . . . . . . . . . . . . 90
Mount Wells . . . . . . . . . . . . . . . . . . . . . . . . . . 94
Metchosin Shoreline . . . . . . . . . . . . . . . . . . . . . . 98
Witty's Lagoon . . . . . . . . . . . . . . . . . . . . . . . . 100
Western Metchosin . . . . . . . . . . . . . . . . . . . . . . 104
Matheson Lake . . . . . . . . . . . . . . . . . . . . . . . . 105
Roche Cove . . . . . . . . . . . . . . . . . . . . . . . . . . 107
East Sooke . . . . . . . . . . . . . . . . . . . . . . . . . . . 112
Sooke Potholes . . . . . . . . . . . . . . . . . . . . . . . . 124
Juan de Fuca Trail . . . . . . . . . . . . . . . . . . . . . . . 140

# Acknowlededgments

In addition to all the contributors to the original volume and the many revisions over the years, for this Thirteenth Edition special thanks are due:

CRD Parks

Saanich Parks

BC Parks

Parks Canada

Municipal staff in Sidney, North Saanich, Central Saanich, Highlands, Saanich, Oak Bay, Victoria, Esquimalt, View Royal, Langford, Colwood, Metchosin, Sooke and various Chambers of Commerce and Tourism Associations from Sidney to Sooke.

Members of various hiking clubs and outdoor organizations and other volunteers, who have provided updates and verified information.

Jim Bisakowski (Desktop Publishing Ltd.) and Lillian Wonders for their advice and expertise.

Photographs courtesy of Richard K. Blier, George Broome, Di Chawner, Joyce Folbigg and Aldyth Hunter.

Finally, special thanks to the VITIS Editorial Committee members, George Broome, John W.E. Harris, Joyce Folbigg, Aldyth Hunter, Shirley Marcetta and to the other society members, Betty Burroughs and Irm Houle.

# A Postscript

To all those both past and present, who had the foresight to recognize the need to preserve the green spaces and unique features of beautiful Vancouver Island, how do we thank you? Parks Canada, BC Parks, Capital Regional District, Saanich Parks, The Land Conservancy, municipalities and the many other agencies who have been involved in the purchase, protection and maintenance of the special natural areas that we enjoy so much. As well, there are the hundreds of individuals who volunteer their time, energy and talent to maintain these areas. What a gift you have given us!

*Vancouver Island Trails Information Society*

# About the Editor
### Richard K. Blier

Outdoor writer, photographer and angler, Richard K. Blier, has explored Vancouver Island's trails, backroads, campsites, lakes and coastlines for over three decades. He is author of three backroad guidebooks: **ISLAND BACKROADS** (Orca Book Publishers, 1998); **MORE ISLAND ADVENTURES** (Orca Book Publishers, 1993); **ISLAND ADVENTURES** (Orca Book Publishers, 1989). He also revised and edited **HIKING TRAILS II** (7$^{th}$ Edition, 1993; 8$^{th}$ Edition, 2000) and **HIKING TRAILS III** (9$^{th}$ Edition, 2002) for the Vancouver Island Trails Information Society. He is a feature writer for **BC OUTDOORS Sports Fishing** and **ISLAND FISHERMAN** magazines. His articles and photos have appeared in newspapers and other books. Please visit BACKROAD ADVENTURES ON VANCOUVER ISLAND at: members.shaw.ca/richardblier.

Photo: Richard K. Blier

# Index

| | | | |
|---|---|---|---|
| About the Editor . . . . . . . . . . . 171 | Elizabeth Mann Park . . . . . . . . 110 |
| Accessible Areas. . . . . . . . . . . 158 | Elk/Beaver Lake 10K Trail . . . . . . 57 |
| Acknowledgments . . . . . . . . . . 169 | Elk/Beaver Lake Regional Park. . . . 57 |
| Albert Head Lagoon Regional Park. . 99 | Elsie King Interpretive Trail . . . . . 53 |
| Albert Head Lagoon Trail. . . . . . . 99 | Endurance Ridge. . . . . . . . . . . 116 |
| Alumni Trail . . . . . . . . . . . . . 69 | Fairy Lake Nature Trail . . . . . . . 137 |
| Anderson Cove . . . . . . . . . . . 114 | Finnerty Gardens . . . . . . . . . . 69 |
| Arbutus Cove Park . . . . . . . . . . 66 | Fires. . . . . . . . . . . . . . . . . 17 |
| Arbutus Ridge. . . . . . . . . . . . 50 | Francis/King Regional Park. . . . . . 53 |
| Arbutus Trail . . . . . . . . . . . . 50 | Freeman King Visitor Centre . . . . . 49 |
| Auburn Trail . . . . . . . . . . . . 91 | French Beach Trail . . . . . . . . . 132 |
| Aylard Farm to Becher Bay . . . . . 114 | Galloping Goose Regional Trail. . . 147 |
| Aylard Farm to Beechey Head . . . 114 | Glencoe Cove-Kwatsech Park . . . . 66 |
| Beach Trail, Devonian. . . . . . . . 103 | Gold Mine Trail. . . . . . . . . . . 50 |
| Beach Trail, Mount Douglas . . . . . 65 | Goldstream Provincial Park. . . . . . 49 |
| Bear Beach, Juan de Fuca Trail . . . 143 | Gore Park . . . . . . . . . . . . . . 39 |
| Bear Hill Regional Park. . . . . . . 58 | Gowlland Tod Provincial Park . . . . 37 |
| Beckwith Park . . . . . . . . . . . 80 | Green Park . . . . . . . . . . . . . 30 |
| Birdwatching . . . . . . . . . . . . 162 | Gulf Islands National Park Reserve. . 21 |
| Blinkhorn Lake Nature Park. . . . . 109 | Harrison Trail . . . . . . . . . . . 126 |
| Bob Mountain Park Trail . . . . . 110 | Henderson Park . . . . . . . . . . . 69 |
| Botanical Beach . . . . . . . . . . 144 | Heritage Grove . . . . . . . . . . . 53 |
| Botanical Beach Loop . . . . . . . . 135 | High Ridge Trail . . . . . . . . . . 54 |
| Buckbrush Swamp Trail . . . . . . . 110 | Hints And Cautions . . . . . . . . . 13 |
| Calypso Trail . . . . . . . . . . . . 91 | Horth Hill Regional Park . . . . . . 29 |
| Camp Barnard . . . . . . . . . . . 128 | How To Use This Book . . . . . . . . 11 |
| Camp Thunderbird. . . . . . . . . 128 | Hyacinth Park. . . . . . . . . . . . 84 |
| Campgrounds . . . . . . . . . . . 157 | Information Sources . . . . . . . . . 167 |
| Cedar Grove Trail . . . . . . . . . . 108 | Iron Mine Bay . . . . . . . . . . . 115 |
| Cedar Hill Golf Course . . . . . . . 73 | Irvine Trail . . . . . . . . . . . . . 63 |
| China Beach to Mystic Beach . . . . 134 | Island View Beach. . . . . . . . . . 155 |
| China Beach to Sombrio Beach . . . 143 | John Dean Provincial Park . . . . . . 33 |
| China Beach Trails . . . . . . . . . 133 | Juan de Fuca Marine Trail. . . . . . 141 |
| Chinese Cemetery. . . . . . . . . . 76 | Kellett Point . . . . . . . . . . . . 108 |
| Christmas Hill Trail. . . . . . . . . 79 | Knockan Hill Park . . . . . . . . . 85 |
| Coast Trail. . . . . . . . . . . . . 115 | Lagoon and Hook Spit . . . . . . . 25 |
| Coles Bay Regional Park . . . . . . 35 | Lagoon Trail. . . . . . . . . . . . 101 |
| Colquitz River Linear Park . . . . . 83 | Layritz Park. . . . . . . . . . . . . 85 |
| Copley Park . . . . . . . . . . . . . 84 | Legend . . . . . . . . . . . . . . . 10 |
| Craigflower Creek Trail. . . . . . . 89 | Lewis J. Clark Trail . . . . . . . . . 87 |
| Cuthbert Holmes Park. . . . . . . . 84 | Lizard Lake Nature Trail . . . . . . 137 |
| D'Arcy Island . . . . . . . . . . . . 26 | Lochside Regional Trail . . . . . . . 153 |
| Devonian Regional Park. . . . . . . 103 | Lone Tree Hill Regional Park. . . . . 46 |
| Dog Regulations . . . . . . . . . . 17 | Lookout Trail . . . . . . . . . . . . 29 |
| Dominion Brook Park. . . . . . . . 34 | Lower Goldstream Trail . . . . . . . 50 |
| Durrance Lake Trail. . . . . . . . . 44 | Maps, List of. . . . . . . . . . . . 168 |
| East Beach and The Bluff. . . . . . 24 | Matheson Creek Trail . . . . . . . . 108 |
| East Sooke Regional Park . . . . . . 113 | Matheson Lake Loop . . . . . . . . 106 |

Matheson Lake Regional Park. . . . 105
McKenzie Bight Trail. . . . . . . . . 44
McKenzie Creek Trail . . . . . . . 88
Merriman Trail . . . . . . . . . . . 64
Metchosin Shoreline . . . . . . . . 99
Metchosin Wilderness Park . . . . . 110
Mill Bay Trail . . . . . . . . . . . 135
Mill Hill Regional Park . . . . . . . 91
Moor Park. . . . . . . . . . . . . 84
Mount Douglas Park . . . . . . . . 63
Mount Finlayson Trail . . . . . . . 50
Mount Maguire . . . . . . . . . . 114
Mount Tolmie Park . . . . . . . . 71
Mount Wells Regional Park. . . . . 95
Mount Work Regional Park. . . . . 43
Mystic Vale, University of Victoria . 69
Nature Walks . . . . . . . . . . . 160
Norn Trail. . . . . . . . . . . . . 65
Oak Haven Park. . . . . . . . . . 39
Panama Hill Park . . . . . . . . . 84
Parkinson Creek to Botanical Beach 144
Parkinson Creek Trail . . . . . . . 135
Pickles Bluff . . . . . . . . . . . 33
Pike Road Trail . . . . . . . . . . 115
Playfair Park . . . . . . . . . . . 80
Portland Island . . . . . . . . . . 21
Postscript . . . . . . . . . . . . 170
Preface . . . . . . . . . . . . . . 4
Prospector's Trail . . . . . . . . . 50
Quick's Bottom . . . . . . . . . . 85
Ridge Trail, Gowlland Tod . . . . . 39
Ridge Trail, Horth Hill . . . . . . . 29
Rithet's Bog Conservation Area. . . . 61
Roche Cove Regional Park . . . . . 107
Rolston Trail . . . . . . . . . . . 61
Ross Bay Cemetery . . . . . . . . . 76
Rowntree Loop . . . . . . . . . . 39
San Juan River Valley Trails . . . . 138
Sandcut Creek Trail . . . . . . . . 133

Sea Bluff Trail. . . . . . . . . . . 102
Seymour Hill Trail . . . . . . . . . 88
Sherwood Pond . . . . . . . . . . 103
Sidney Spit . . . . . . . . . . . . 24
Sombrio Beach to Parkinson Creek . 144
Sombrio Beach Trail. . . . . . . . 134
Sooke Hills Wilderness
    Regional Park Reserve. . . . . . 96
Sooke Mountain Provincial Park . . 126
Sooke Potholes Provincial Park . . . 125
Sooke Potholes Regional Park. . . . 125
Suggested Reading . . . . . . . . 165
Summit Trail . . . . . . . . . . . 43
Swan Creek Park . . . . . . . . . 85
Swan Lake Loop . . . . . . . . . . 79
Swan Lake/Christmas Hill Nature
    Sanctuary . . . . . . . . . . . 79
Thetis Lake Regional Park . . . . . 87
Thetis Lake to Scafe Hill . . . . . . 88
Timberman Trail . . . . . . . . . . 38
Tod Inlet . . . . . . . . . . . . . 38
Tower Point . . . . . . . . . . . . 100
Trillium Trail . . . . . . . . . . . 88
Two Lake Loop . . . . . . . . . . 88
University of Victoria. . . . . . . . 69
Upper Goldstream Trail. . . . . . . 50
Valley Mist Trail . . . . . . . . . . 34
Vancouver Island Trails
    Information Society . . . . . . . 19
Victoria Waterfront . . . . . . . . . 75
Wayne's Rock Trail . . . . . . . . 111
West Coast Road:
    Sooke to Port Renfrew. . . . . . 131
West Coast Trail. . . . . . . . . . 145
West Viewpoint. . . . . . . . . . . 34
Western Metchosin . . . . . . . . 105
Whiffin Spit Park . . . . . . . . . 121
Whittaker Trail . . . . . . . . . . 64
Wildlife: Bears and Cougars . . . . 16
Witty's Lagoon Regional Park . . . 100

# Trail & Nature Notes